The University & Urban Revival

THE CITY IN THE **21st** CENTURY

Eugenie L. Birch and Susan M. Wachter,
Series Editors

A complete list
of books in the series
is available from the publisher.

JUDITH RODIN

The University & Urban Revival

Out of the Ivory Tower and Into the Streets

PENN

UNIVERSITY OF PENNSYLVANIA PRESS

PHILADELPHIA

Published by
University of Pennsylvania Press
Philadelphia, Pennsylvania 19104-4112

Printed in the United States of America on acid-free paper
10 9 8 7 6 5 4 3 2

Library of Congress Cataloging-in-Publication Data

Rodin, Judith.
    The university and urban revival: out of the ivory tower and into the streets / Judith Rodin.
        p. cm. — (The city in the twenty-first century)
    Includes bibliographical references and index.
    ISBN-13: 978-0-8122-4022-1 [(hardcover): alk. paper]
    ISBN-10: 0-8122-4022-7 [(hardcover): alk. paper]
1. Urban renewal—Pennsylvania—Philadelphia. 2. Community and college—Pennsylvania—
Philadelphia. 3. University of Pennsylvania—Public services. I. University of Pennsylvania.
II. Title.
    HT177.P47R63 2007
    307.3'4160974811—dc22   2007017899

No single element in a city is, in truth, the kingpin or the key. The mixture itself is kingpin, and its mutual support is in the order. A city's very structure consists of a mixture of uses, and we get closest to its structural secrets when we deal with the conditions that generate **diversity**.

— JANE JACOBS

CONTENTS

PROLOGUE

No ONE WHO lived in West Philadelphia at the time will ever forget what happened on the night of October 31, 1996. The weather had been ideal for trick-or-treating and as the cool, clear evening drew to a close, the neighborhood near the University of Pennsylvania campus tucked itself in. Just a few hours earlier, the tree-lined streets were bustling with pint-sized ghosts and ballerinas. Parents chatted with one another while they waited for their young charges to collect Halloween goodies in shopping bags crammed with chocolates and candy corn, or sugarless bubblegum from the more nutrition-conscious families who populated the eclectic urban neighborhood. Many in this neighborhood were urban pioneers, committed to inner-city living and the ideal of racial and economic diversity. Others had resided in the area for years, unable to move. The mix of blue-collar workers, academics, artists, and families on welfare represented most inner-city urban neighborhoods surrounding universities.

Shortly before 11 p.m., Vladimir Sled, a thirty-eight-year-old Russian émigré and Penn biochemist who often worked late in his lab at the medical school, left for home with his fiancée, coworker Cecilia Hagerhall. As they strolled toward their apartment in West Philadelphia, passing under a bright street light, they were accosted by robbers who attempted to grab Hagerhall's purse and punched her. Sled intervened to stop the assault. During the ensuing struggle, Sled was stabbed multiple times. Neighbors heard Hagerhall's screams and when they arrived on the scene, they found her holding her bleeding boyfriend. Vladimir Sled died shortly afterward at the University of Pennsylvania medical center, leaving behind his bereft fiancée and a twelve-year-old son who was visiting his dad that week. Sled's death not only horrified the campus and the community; it shocked an entire city.

A rash of attacks—nearly thirty armed robberies on or near the campus in a particularly brutal September, including the shooting of an undergraduate who fortunately survived his wounds—had already mobilized the University to increase security once again. Only two years before, one month after I arrived as president, Penn graduate student and gifted mathematician Al-Moez Alimohamed was fatally gunned down for pocket change about seven blocks from campus in August 1994. For the next year, my first as president, Alimohamed's father and brother relentlessly appealed to me to "do something" to make the area safer. What made it even more painful was that I knew the family of the victim's bereaved girlfriend, Rebecca Rosen. When Rebecca committed suicide in 1995, her death haunted me then as it does to this day. Her father begged me, as Alimohamed's family had done, to do something to restore peace and security in the neighborhood.

In the wake of these events, campus and community safety demanded immediate attention. We fired the University's commissioner of public safety, hired an experienced captain from the Philadelphia Police Department to replace him, and developed a sophisticated, multi-pronged public safety plan. Yet, two years later, we had to ask how these efforts could have failed.

Sometimes, there is one decisive moment—one seminal incident—that leaves no choice but to seek an entirely new paradigm. With the events of that Halloween night—a random act of violence in a neighborhood that had become increasingly rife with crime—that moment was foisted on me. As President of University of Pennsylvania, I knew that the time for unprecedented action had arrived.

The University & Urban Revival

CHAPTER 1

Mobilizing for Action

MORE THAN HALF of the nation's colleges and universities are located in cities. They represent significant contributors to the character of their cities and to the definition of the urban environment. By virtue of their mission, intellectual capital, and investments in physical facilities, urban universities and their medical centers are uniquely positioned to play a leading role in their communities in powerful ways.

Yet urban universities have not typically been the most agreeable neighbors. At best, their involvement with adjacent communities has been intermittent and inconsistent. For decades these institutions have flexed their huge muscles of property ownership and pushed their way into the surrounding areas. The all-too-familiar cycle of depopulated urban neighborhoods and resultant increase in crime, which in turn made a neighborhood even less desirable, had its beginnings in the 1950s with "white flight" to the suburbs. The ensuing urban-renewal projects of the 1960s increased the dissension between town and gown as disgruntled homeowners were displaced to make room for the expansion of these institutions with newly available federal urban-renewal dollars. Then, as the funds dried up and the neighborhoods around them deteriorated, academic and medical institutions turned inward, preferring to remain insulated rather than address the problems in their own backyards. When there were institutional attempts at developing better community relationships, they were most often inadequate, lacking sustainable changes and solutions. And so the cycle continued.

The situation of the neighborhood surrounding the University of Pennsylvania campus in the 1990s exemplified these issues. The whole of West Philadelphia, the broad contiguous section that encompasses University City, had been in a state of serious decline since the 1950s. From the mid- to late 1980s, the area had become increasingly blighted and unsafe. One in five residents had income below the poverty line. Shops and businesses were closing, pedestrian traffic was vanishing, middle-class families were leaving, and more houses were falling prey to abandonment and decay. The streets were littered with trash, and abandoned homes and buildings became canvases for graffiti artists and business addresses for drug dealers.

The public schools were in especially bad shape. They were overcrowded and antiquated, and three local elementary schools ranked at the bottom in state-administered math and reading tests. The main commercial thoroughfare through Penn's campus was dominated by surface parking lots, while the depressed and desolate commercial corridor of 40th Street at the western edge of Penn's campus had become an invisible boundary beyond which many Penn students and faculty dared not venture. And despite the efforts of some faculty and administrators to reach out to the community, the relationship between the University and the community was testy, to say the least. Residents by and large felt that Penn had turned its back on the neighborhood.

Who could blame them? Penn was so near and loomed large, yet felt so remote. The city's largest private employer spent hundreds of millions of dollars a year on goods, services, and construction, yet little of that trickled down to local businesses. Penn operated commercial real estate with seemingly little regard for what kinds of businesses were leasing its properties. Some establishments, like the local fast-food eatery, were especially seedy and menacing. If quality of life means all those aspects of the environment—physical, economic, and social—that make a community a desirable place in which to live or do business, then Penn was not only failing to do its part to enhance the quality of life in the neighborhood but was also, albeit unwittingly, contributing to its decline. Even the University buildings kept their distance, with windowless walls of brick or stone facing the street and forming a fortresslike barrier.

The issue of mending its deteriorating relations with the community and revitalizing West Philadelphia had long been on Penn's agenda, and many efforts had been made. But when the problem of security was driven once again to the forefront, we had to find an entirely new model for action. One unforgettable meeting that stiffened my resolve to search for new paradigms and sustainable solutions took place just a few weeks after Vladimir Sled's murder in the fall of 1996. It was Family Weekend on campus, and we held a previously scheduled open forum on safety issues. Some five hundred parents attended and grilled me about my administration's efforts to safeguard their children. Understandably, the atmosphere was heated—the parents were angry, terrified, consumed with worry. A few threatened to pull their children out of school. I highlighted the safety initiatives I had announced that fall, outlined the University's safety-related programs, and discussed our plans for new residences and retail spaces to draw student activity back onto campus. At one point, the irate crowd booed the very popular Mayor Ed Rendell (the city's former district attorney and a Penn alum) when he tried to discuss possible solutions to crime besides a heightened police presence, ones that involved their children's behavior. The booing was not restricted to the mayor. My response, however, was equally vehement. I reminded the parents that we were in this together and that we shared a mutual need and desire for our students to be safe. I meant every word, because I, too, was a parent. My son and stepson lived with my husband and me in the president's house on the western edge of the campus.

The president's house at 3812 Walnut Street is an elegant French chateau, built for West Philadelphia cigar manufacturer Otto C. Eisenlohr in 1912 and renovated in 1982. The house is considered one of the gems of architect Horace Trumbauer's career. Life was comfortable in that wonderfully grand classical mansion conveniently located within minutes of my office, but it was in bizarre juxtaposition to the neighborhood around it. The nearest grocery store was many blocks away, and it was often plagued by long lines at the checkout and by inadequate food quality, with prices reflecting the lack of competition. There was no place to buy a new sweater or a nice birthday gift. There were few restaurants. And I confess that the dark, empty streets made everyone jumpy. Having school-age children, I could relate to what every West Philadelphia parent felt about the safety of the area and the lack of good educational options.

When I assumed the presidency, my son, Alex, was in seventh grade and my stepson, Gibson, was in tenth grade. As a product of public schools, I have always been fully committed to public-school education. It was with tremendous dismay that my husband and I decided to send the boys to private schools. But in light of the failing neighborhood schools, private school seemed the only option for many University City parents. Each weekday morning, more than fifteen buses crisscrossed West Philadelphia, transporting neighborhood children to private and parochial schools throughout the city and the western suburbs. Because our sons did not attend neighborhood schools, their friends were dispersed throughout the city and the surrounding towns. We were not the only family with these issues—similar scenes were routine in many households across University City. And we were the lucky ones. Most West Philadelphia parents lacked cars and money for private schools.

The streets of University City did not feel safe. The dearth of public parks and green spaces left parents no choice but to push strollers through broken glass, litter, and sometimes discarded drug paraphernalia in the few parks that did exist. Vladimir Sled's murder was the last straw.

The University had been working on community relations for a decade, and there had been progress and improvements in the neighborhood. We had instituted many new safety measures and had invested heavily in security. Now there was an urgent need to accomplish broader and more sweeping change at warp speed. Two years before, when Alimohamed was murdered, I was unsure that we had the resources or the institutional will to accomplish holistic change on a neighborhood-wide scale. The stakes were even higher now. It was apparent that we were going to have to invest huge amounts of creativity, time, and money in an integrated, broad, community-development effort.

We could no longer rely on the great efforts of faculty to work in West Philadelphia if doing so fitted within their research purview. We could no longer feel good about encouraging students and staff to volunteer in the local schools, or about several of our smaller community-improvement initiatives. We had to face the prospect of taking the lead in redeveloping a distressed neighborhood that disliked us and of assuming an unprecedented level of financial and social risk.

Many have asked what other factors contributed to my personal passion and depth of commitment to the revitalization of West Philadelphia. After all, when I accepted the presidency, I was going to lead an Ivy League school with an outstanding faculty of academic scholars and leaders in their respective fields. Penn students were bright, creative, and intellectually curious. My job description did not include transforming the neighborhood.

I suppose it was only natural that some questioned whether my role as the first female president of an Ivy League university influenced me to push the West Philadelphia initiatives. Of course, I was aware that my leadership would be especially scrutinized because of my gender. While I knew that there was no one particular style of "female leadership" and that ultimately my leadership would be judged by my accomplishments, perhaps I was more determined to fix the neighborhood because I was a woman and a mother. And certainly my commitment to the revitalization of West Philadelphia had to do with deep affection for the city and the neighborhood in which I had grown up and for the credibility of my alma mater, which had been so critical in shaping my life. It was also an outgrowth of political activism, formulated early in my education and further encouraged at Penn, where I honed leadership skills in student government. And it grew out of a lifetime of living and working in urban areas and an appreciation for the intellectual excitement and cultural stimulation—as well as the considerable challenges—they offered.

After graduating from Penn, I continued my doctoral studies in psychology at Columbia University. With that move, my political and social awareness increased in quantum leaps as I found myself in the midst of campus turmoil unlike anything I had experienced before. Recall that Columbia in the 1960s experienced the most significant crisis in its history, placing the Morningside Heights campus in the national spotlight. The currents of unrest sweeping the nation—opposition to the Vietnam War, an increasingly militant civil-rights movement, and the ongoing decline of America's inner cities—all converged in a chaotic upheaval at Columbia. In the last week of April 1968, more than a thousand protesting students occupied five buildings, effectively shutting down the university until they were forcibly removed by the New York City police.

I closely observed the mediation between Columbia administrators and students who had taken over university buildings to protest the razing of a decaying neighborhood to put up a gymnasium. Those tumultuous events led to the cancellation of the proposed gym in Morningside Park, the termination of certain classified research projects, the retirement of President Grayson Kirk, and a slump in Columbia's finances and morale. They also led to the creation of the University Senate, in which faculty, students, and alumni acquired a larger voice in university affairs.

Witnessing the confrontation between authority figures (whether police or university administrators) and students, who passionately voiced their beliefs, was a tutorial in human behavior. I saw that violence can arise from a clash between strongly held beliefs and a system that does not seem to get it. Ultimately, the system did respond, but a healthy, engaged dialogue would have accomplished more. It was a lesson I would never forget.

With an offer to teach at Yale, I moved to New Haven, where I remained for the next twenty-two years, the last two as provost. New

Haven was experiencing the same pangs of turmoil as many other cities throughout the country. The community was still suffering the effects of the riots of the summer of '67, a backlash against the federal government's shift away from aiding the poor and helping those living in the inner city. While the participants in the riots during those two days were a minority of the population in the neighborhood where the incidents occurred, it was evident that political leaders had failed to recognize that this minority represented the voice of the majority. Once again, I saw how critical it was to be in tune with the community and to respond in kind. Another lesson was imprinted on me for the future.

At Yale I also became familiar with Jane Jacobs's seminal work, *The Death and Life of Great American Cities* (1961), which scoffed at much of the urban planning of the twentieth century and instead offered a studied, considered observation of the features that ultimately make and keep a city livable.[1] My perspective on urban life was hugely influenced by Jacobs's remarkable book. From these myriad influences, it became clear to me that the leaders of cities needed help in enhancing, reviving, and reaffirming urbanism as a critical feature of American life. Little did I know I would be called upon to act, to test this crucible of commitment in the aftermath of violence.

I was thrilled and honored in 1994 to return to Penn as president and to my hometown. In my Freshman Convocation speech that year, I pointed out the greatness of the city: "Within a five-mile radius of the campus, you will find a world-class art museum, a renowned orchestra, a marvelous zoo, a celebrated planetarium and natural history museum as well as world-class restaurants, shopping and entertainment. Philadelphia is also the place where the two most important documents in American history—the Constitution and the Declaration of Independence—were debated, drafted, and signed. In short, Philadelphia is a vibrant, exciting city. Yet within a five-mile radius of the campus, there are communities where unemployment is high, housing is deteriorated, and where children struggle to escape from poverty and neglect. In Philadelphia, you will see the most vivid of contrasts between high culture and devastating poverty. And yet both are part of Penn."

I spoke too about what had drawn me back to Penn: "Penn has always been for me a place where ideas generated tremendous excitement, and where intellectual and social life flowed together seamlessly. It was the place where I learned to think well, to be bold and take chances, to challenge old paradigms. It was, above all, a place deeply committed to the open and free expression of new ideas of all kinds."

But exhilarating as it was to return to Penn, it was also devastating to see how much the surrounding area had deteriorated. The neighborhoods I remembered as adjoining the campus no longer existed. Gone was the vitality I recalled, which was all the more distressing because my memories of growing up on 59th and Windsor streets were particularly wonderful. The Cobbs Creek area in Southwest Philadelphia, where we had lived, had been a lower-middle-class neighborhood of row houses inhabited by a tightly knit mix of Jewish and Catholic families. We did not have much, nor did we really want much. Everything we needed was nearby. The neighborhood seemed like a paradise for kids. In fact, until I started elementary school, I did not know many children from around the corner on Warrington Street because we had enough kids on our street for a baseball game. It did not get any better than that!

So with my responsibilities as president, and the distinct history and advantage I had of being a hometown kid who was a product of the Philadelphia public schools and a Penn alum, I built on my experiences as an observer of the power and the decay of American cities. It was a privilege to lead Penn as it sought to become a catalyst for neighborhood transformation. The goal was to build capacity back into a deeply distressed inner-city neighborhood—*educational* capacity, *retail* capacity, *quality-of-life* capacity, and especially *economic* capacity. We demolished literal and figurative walls that kept Penn and its neighbors from forging nourishing connections with one another. We restructured buildings and open spaces to make the campus "more like seams and less like barriers" to the community, as Jacobs had advocated.[2] And we worked to unite "town and gown" as one richly diverse community that could learn, grow, socialize, and live together in a safe, flourishing, and economically sustainable urban environment.

As I wrote this book, I was haunted by images of the victims of Hurricane Katrina in New Orleans—poor people, largely black, who were literally left behind. America is reaching out for new solutions. In a trenchant *New York Times* op-ed piece, David Brooks comments:

> Especially in these days after Katrina, everybody laments poverty and inequality. But what are you doing about it? For example, let's say you work at a university or a college. You are a cog in one of the great inequality producing machines this country has known. What are you doing to change that?[3]

This book describes one university's answer.

CHAPTER 2

Why Neighborhood Revitalization

In the past few decades, it has become increasingly difficult for urban colleges and universities to turn their backs on the problems of their cities, because these institutions cannot deny that the cities' troubles have become their own as well. Many cities, suffering from the press of poverty, crime, and physical deterioration, have called upon the academic institutions in their midst for help. A few university presidents stepped up early to take on major civic leadership roles and responsibilities (such as Richard Atkinson, chancellor of the University of California, San Diego; Evan Dobelle, president of Trinity College in Hartford; and Carl Patton, president of Georgia State University in Atlanta).

Strong civic leadership should be expected to emerge from urban academic institutions. In *The Wealth of Cities*, former four-term mayor of Milwaukee John O. Norquist writes, "The best institutions of education in the world are usually located in cities. The size, diversity, and density of cities create a natural advantage attractive to consumers of education. In the United States, the urban education advantage can clearly be seen in higher education."[1]

Not only do cities attract "consumers of education." Urban academic institutions in turn have a tremendous economic impact on their cities. From the late nineteenth century through the mid-twentieth, industry, financial institutions, and public utilities were typically the largest employers in most American cities. In recent decades, however, as manufacturing jobs moved out of cities and as banks and public utilities consolidated, universities and their associated medical centers have grown to become the largest employers in a surprising number of cities. In every one of the twenty largest cities in the United States, an institution of higher education or an academic medical center is among the top ten private employers, despite differences among these cities in age, region, and development pattern. Thirty-five percent of the people who work for private employers in these cities are employed by universities and their medical centers. And in four of the cities—Washington, D.C., Philadelphia, San Diego, and Baltimore—institutions of higher learning ("eds") and medical facilities ("meds") account for more than half of the jobs generated.[2]

These are impressive data. They tell us that eds and meds are fueling the economy in their cities, as employers and as enormous consumers of goods and services. Ira Harkavy and Harmon Zuckerman, in a 1999 survey of eds and meds as employers, viewed these institutions as one of the often overlooked fixed assets of cities and as potential boons to the local economy.[3] In addition to job creation and purchasing power, these institutions conduct research and impart intellectual resources and technical expertise to their cities. They contribute to a more experienced and educated workforce. Their economic activities foster an entrepreneurial spirit and attract additional economic growth. A full measure of their economic impact includes the compounding of benefits that result when employee salaries and supplier payments are spent successively for additional purchases or salaries. This indirect economic ripple, which economists describe as the "multiplier effect," can create billions of dollars of additional economic activity.

A call for unleashing the local economic development capacity of these institutions as a national priority was made by the Initiative for a Competitive Inner City and CEOs for Cities in their joint study.[4] They present data showing that, for example, in 1996, the more than nineteen hundred urban-core universities in the United States collectively employed two million workers and spent $136 billion in salaries, goods, and services. They note that this was nine times greater than federal direct spending that same year on urban businesses and job development. They comment on how well positioned these institutions are to focus on inner cities in particular.

Universities also have powerful social and intellectual impact on their cities and regions. They provide cultural resources that often serve large public audiences. Attractions associated with universities, including musical performances, art shows, and lectures, stimulate ideas and energize people ranging from local schoolchildren to older, continuing learners. When a university channels its intellectual power and creativity, it has the potential to create a valuable dynamic that is mutually beneficial to the university and the community.

As highlighted by Richard Palm and J. Douglas Toma, "the role of the metropolitan university is not just to be in the city but to be in partnership with the city."[5] When one considers the multitude of opportunities for strong university-city partnerships, the potential is enormous. And one of the greatest advantages for students (those "consumers of education") at urban institutions, in particular, is the opportunity to expand academic learning by bridging the gap between theoretical work in the classroom and practical real-world issues and challenges that cities present. This is education at its best.

There is a newly emerging body of research on universities playing various civic roles; two recent reviews have analyzed an array of such case studies. The Joint Study by the Institute for a Competitive Inner City and CEOs for Cities[6] focused more on universities' potential as agents of local economic development, and the other review (edited by David Perry and Wim Wiewel)[7] highlighted the university as urban real-estate developer. While both include Penn among their examples, it is not alone. Other institutions helping to rebuild community assets in their cities include Georgia State University, Trinity, Yale, Columbia, Howard, Virginia Commonwealth University, the University of Southern California, the University of Illinois (Chicago), and the University of Pittsburgh, as well as the University of Chicago, which undertook the earliest and most well known effort to improve the appearance, safety, and socioeconomic quality of its local neighborhood. (Perry and Wiewel and the Joint Study by Initiative for a Competitive Inner City and CEOs for Cities provide extensive descriptions of many of these efforts; I shall discuss only a few examples.)

Howard University is an excellent case in point. In response to criticism about its neglected real-estate holdings, Howard paired with the Washington, D.C., government, Fannie Mae, and corporate partners to transform forty-five properties in a crime-ridden neighborhood into more than three hundred housing units and $65 million in commercial development. Another institution that has assumed an active role in transforming its community is Virginia Commonwealth University, which formed a joint venture with the state of Virginia and the city of Richmond to create the Virginia Bio-Technology Research Park. Out of this successful center, twenty-six companies have been created—with VCU faculty research accounting for 75 percent of them. And in an effort to generate job growth, Columbia University has joined with the Morningside Area Alliance to create the Job Connections Program to identify, screen, and refer job candidates to Columbia and other large local institutions in the Morningside area.

In addition, Perry and Wiewel's review demonstrates, the urban real-estate development practices of universities represent one of their most important institutional practices.[8] Since a fundamental tension often exists between the university as campus and its neighboring community, these institutional practices are frequently called into question by their critics. Two articles in the *Chronicle of Higher Education* by Paul Fain and Richard Freeland, respectively, refer to Penn's real estate and economic development efforts as a "national model of constructive town-gown interaction and partnership," a theme echoed—after decades of criticism—by the *Philadelphia Inquirer* in a special report on life in University City and in the *Washington Post*, among others.[9]

Such results were many years in coming. But beginning in 1996, in concert with the community, the city government, and numerous public and private stakeholders, Penn engaged in a multipronged strategy designed to effect broad, systemic change by undertaking multiple domains of redevelopment and revitalization simultaneously. No single model for wide-scale, university-led urban redevelopment existed when we began our work, although we and others had been at it for a long time. Instead, the revitalization effort that became known as the West Philadelphia Initiatives was guided by a newly developed master strategy that emerged from studying the social, political, and economic forces at work on the ground in West Philadelphia, and in decayed urban neighborhoods generally, and from an evaluation of urban-planning and economic-development theory.

This book examines the economic and social changes that Penn sought to achieve by operating holistically and with long-term commitment to the redevelopment of its local community. It describes the multiple facets of the integrated neighborhood revitalization strategy Penn undertook, the leveraging of resources for economic and retail development, improved housing and increased housing options, improvements in local schools spearheaded by the construction of a university-assisted public school, and new ideas for making the area clean and safe. In telling this story, I hope to show how the University played its roles as agent of change and investor, and to illustrate the impact that a university can make when it accepts that its destiny is entwined with that of its neighbors.

I saw firsthand the value of reconnecting universities with their cities and communities. Penn's engagement with its neighbors has had a regenerating effect both on the neighborhood and on the University. Faculty members became energized in their search for new ways to bring knowledge and experience to bear on urban problems locally and beyond. I vividly remember when mathematics department chair Dennis DeTurck told me, a few years into these initiatives, that if anyone had told him ten years earlier that he would be writing a National Science Foundation proposal for funding to test the new math curriculum he was to implement in our local K-12 schools, he would surely have thought them crazy. Throughout the University, in all its departments and schools, many faculty members became substantively, deeply engaged. This was no longer scholarship *about* the community; this was scholarship *for* the community, its needs, and its potential.

Not only did these efforts challenge and capture the scholarly imagination of many of the faculty, they became a competitive advantage in the recruitment of different types of students, those who were turned on by the ideas and passion this commitment represented. Penn already attracted excellent students, with thousands more applicants than we could admit. But what lessons, other than the rich learning of academic disciplines and professions, did we want to teach them?

We came to believe that we could better educate and exhort talented students to contribute to society and become leaders if we offered them an institutional example of positive civic engagement. If Penn could make discoveries that contributed to saving lives and driving the global economy, then surely we could demonstrate both the capacity and the moral obligation to use our intellectual might to make things right at our doorstep. The willingness of universities and their neighbors to participate in the conversations of democracy—something that is rarely smooth and rarely easy—is the only way to gain the long-term benefits of mutual trust and understanding. How a university performs this civic role serves as an example to its students.

In part, the answer we chose was a response to the question "What is a university?" posed by John Henry Newman, the great English theologian, in his polemic on the nature and scope of university education more than 150 years ago. Newman wrote that a university is "a place where inquiry is pushed forward, and discoveries perfected and verified."[10] We believed, as Cardinal Newman did, that all knowledge is connected and that the success of our efforts would be a manifestation of this belief, incorporating Penn's intellectual resources from across the disciplines and applying them to the revitalization effort.

Another view, from apartheid-era South Africa, speaks to this issue. Included in the book *Letters from Robben Island* is a letter in which Ahmed Kathrada, a political prisoner with Nelson Mandela, wrote to a friend during his ordeal, "Tell my family, I'm not in prison, but in a university."[11] I doubt that his words were hyperbole, or for that matter merely an attempt to calm his parents. After all, a university is where people learn from one another, communicate, and think, and can exist, for some, even as part of a chain gang chipping away at rock. And just as a prison can be a university, so too can a university be a prison, whose bars are orthodoxy or indifference. It is not enough for us to produce brilliant, imaginative doctors, lawyers, scholars, and scientists who will push the envelopes of their disciplines or professions; we must also engage them in the large issues of our day, in the ferment of our times and our society, and in the issues in our own backyard.

In *Measuring Up 2000: The State-by-State Report Card for Higher Education*, Thomas Ehrlich, a founding board member of the National Center for Public Policy and Higher Education, wrote: "Campuses should not be expected to promote a single type of civic or political engagement, but they should prepare their graduates to become engaged citizens who provide the time, attention, understanding, and action to further collective civic goals. Institutions of higher education should help students to recognize themselves as members of a larger social fabric, to consider social problems to be at least partly their own, to see the civic dimensions of issues, to make and justify informed civic judgments, and to take action when appropriate."[12]

These days there is much talk that cynicism is pervading the American spirit, that people are losing faith in institutions, that they are coming to believe that action and involvement are futile. Just look at politics. Some wonder why anyone would want to enter that mean-spirited and dispirited arena. Look at the media. Why would anyone want to join a profession that often seems to wish to hasten our destruction just so it can report on it? While I certainly have heard the cynics and I have listened to the silence of the indifferent, that is not all I have heard across the nation's campuses. I have listened to students speak with compassion about the plight of children in urban ghettos and have watched them respond with zealous action. I have heard faculty explain their research with passion and watched the search for new ways to make teaching a more inspiring experience. I have seen the loyal dedication of staff members to both the ideals of education and the care of "their" students and faculty. Furthermore, I have been moved by neighbors reaching out for partnerships in our communities. These were the underpinnings we sought to connect.

Penn and other urban universities are making progress in learning how to revive and celebrate deep and real civic engagement as a key feature of life in the United States. But we must understand that this progress requires regular nourishment. Although the conversations are often difficult, they must never stop. I am convinced that sustained community partnerships will help define successful universities in the twenty-first century; without a continuous civic dialogue, such partnerships will fail, and both the universities and their neighborhood will suffer.

In the course of working to revitalize West Philadelphia, we raised the bar on our level of commitment to the community as we strove to achieve a level of civic engagement that was strategic, comprehensive, intense, and purposeful. Our strategy depended on new ideas and new partners, significant resources, and a long-range view toward sustainability. Although we began planning and working on all of the initiatives simultaneously, we made a pointed decision not to announce a sweeping effort. We knew from past experience and from the community-development literature that this was not something the University could do *to* the neighborhood or even *for* the neighborhood. This was something Penn had to do *in concert with* the community, working with its residents and its activists, community associations and city officials, and University administrators, students, and faculty. What was needed was extensive and continuous consultation, not formal announcements.

As we consulted, we also turned to urban theory to inform our thinking. The 1990s had yielded valuable lessons about urban revitalization, offering new and exciting ideas of urbanism. We were especially influenced by Andrés Duany and Elizabeth Plater-Zyberk, founders of the New Urbanism movement, who assert that a vibrant public realm makes cities so appealing. They design active streets to transform deteriorating areas into thriving twenty-four-hour-a-day neighborhoods with shopping and other amenities within walking distance from dwellings. And with each project, they insist on an intense form of public involvement in the design process. They firmly believe that to revive a deteriorating area, it is critical to create a *process of revival.*

That process of revival, the very definition of public engagement, goes far beyond consulting alone. Roberta Gratz and Norman Mintz suggest the importance of "urban husbandry" as well—the "tender tweaking" provided by actively involved and committed residents and stakeholders that is critical to overall success.[13] Included in this tweaking is planting gardens, replacing broken streetlights, removing graffiti. This is a critical component of the change effort, because it provides a basis of energy and creativity for further change. And people more easily become committed if they see the involvement of others like them. As David Boehlke observes, social fabric is as important as a strong economy for healthy neighborhoods to develop.[14]

It was also clear that many theorists and planners were arguing powerfully for an integrated approach that tackled many elements simultaneously. Elise Bright refers to the "urban web" that must be addressed to determine quality of life in a neighborhood and ensure successful revitalization.[15] And as Ross Gittell and Avis Vidal note, a holistic approach reflects the expectation that addressing several dimensions of community life in a coordinated way will be synergistic.[16] For example, David Varady and Jeffrey Raffel argue that along with housing rehabilitation and increased homeownership, dealing with schools and crime are key to restoring declining neighborhoods.[17] Michael Greenberg's "hierarchy of needs" for improving neighborhood quality placed essential amenities, such as police and fire protection and garbage-collection services, at the top of the ladder.[18] Greenberg found that irrespective of other characteristics, a neighborhood gets a rating of poor or fair quality when both crime and serious blight are present. This understanding, coupled with the increase of crime in the neighborhood, underscored our resolve to jumpstart the revitalization efforts with a "clean and safe" initiative.

Ultimately, the lesson that we took from our review was that, with regard to urban revitalization, the likelihood for success is greater if two factors are present: integrated synergistic intervention and good communications and partnerships. No one institution has the resources or tools to solve all the problems facing inner-city neighborhoods. Neighbors need a reason to continue to invest their time, energy, and dollars in the neighborhood. Government must play a critical role in the development of affordable housing, licensing and inspection practices, and tax abatements for private-sector initiatives. Foundations and the private sector must be shown compelling reasons to invest.

But ultimately some entity with enough commitment and skin in the game to have credibility and clout has to lead, to leverage these multiple resources most effectively. For Penn this leadership had to be gentle, such was the history of decades of mistrust between the community, the city, and the University. A different kind of leadership was required for a new type of broad and deep engagement. This meant not only new ways of dealing with our stakeholders and prospective partners but also new ways of organizing ourselves to take on this ambitious and far-reaching effort. With great deliberation, we developed a rationale for planning and structures to implement the plans. The West Philadelphia Initiatives specified five integrated goals:

1. improve neighborhood safety, services, and capacities;
2. provide high-quality, diverse housing choices;
3. revive commercial activity;
4. accelerate economic development; and
5. enhance local public school options.

But before delving into these, it is useful to understand the history of Penn and West Philadelphia, a history familiar to, and an exemplar of, most urban universities in America.

CHAPTER 3

The Growth of University City

SOMETIMES THE SEEMINGLY most insignificant happenings render the most satisfaction. That's how it was when Penn's W. E. B. Du Bois College House (the residential community whose "living-learning" program focuses on the African and African American experience) hosted the annual performance of the historical-fiction play *Taking a Stand: A Black Bottom Workshop Performance* in 1999. After several years of the play's being staged off-campus, the change of venue was probably not very significant to the casual theatergoer. But for Penn, it was especially noteworthy. The play commemorates the destruction of the Black Bottom neighborhood, a dynamic African American working-class community of row houses and businesses in West Philadelphia. Under the guise of 1960s urban renewal that would expand Penn's holdings in the area, this community was decimated. The willingness to perform the workshop on campus with a cast of students, community members, and former neighborhood residents signaled that the longstanding tension between the University and the community was finally abating. Peace had been a long time coming.

The history of the growth and expansion of Penn, and indeed of most urban universities, is rife with the kind of aggressive bulldozing that destroyed the Black Bottom area in the name of progress. Certainly much of the development was meant ultimately to improve the neighborhood, in part by making it attractive to faculty and students, but the process was, at best, misguided and often arrogant. Penn's actions toward its neighbors hardly reflected the values of its founder, Benjamin Franklin. The reality for urban universities, whose infrastructures root them in densely populated areas, has been that growth could be achieved only through encroachment on, and often destruction of, surrounding neighborhoods. Yet, for urban institutions to thrive, room to grow remains a critical issue.

The mantra of today's real-estate market—location, location, location—had just as much import in colonial Philadelphia when Ben Franklin sought to find a site for a college whose ideas for practical and theoretical learning he had laid out in a widely read pamphlet. In a city center as densely populated as Philadelphia's was in the eighteenth century, affordable properties were hard to come by. At the time, Franklin happened to be a trustee of the Great Hall, a building at 4th and Arch streets erected (with Franklin's financial help) by supporters of the Reverend George Whitefield. Whitefield was the most popular charismatic of the roving preachers of the Great Awakening, the religious revivalist movement sweeping the colonies, and his call for humanitarianism appealed to Franklin. When the movement began to wane, Franklin, ever the businessman, negotiated a deal for the Great Hall to house a school. And so it was that the Publick Academy of Philadelphia, the first nonsectarian college in America and the school that was to become the University of Pennsylvania, opened in January 1751 in a choice location, thanks to its wily founder.

Could Franklin have imagined that someday his small academy would become one of the country's great research universities? Certainly his ambition was to lay the groundwork for a secular institution that would some day rival the four elite religious colleges of the time, Harvard, William and Mary, Yale, and Princeton. But he could not have foreseen the rancor that his school would create in future centuries in its quest for prominence.

Today, Penn's West Philadelphia campus covers almost three hundred acres and is home to 151 buildings (excluding the hospitals). Total enrollment for 2005–06 topped twenty-three thousand. Women make up 51 percent of all students enrolled, and the faculty number more than four thousand. With more than twenty-four thousand employees at the University and Penn Medicine, Penn is today the largest private employer in the city of Philadelphia.

A brief look at the institution's history of physical growth unravels the threads of growing dissention in the community, although Penn's first effort at expansion a half-century after its founding was relatively uneventful. The University had moved five blocks west, to 9th and Chestnut streets, into a large building originally intended to be a residence for the president of the United States.[1] In what was perhaps a prescient decision, Penn demolished the President's House in 1829 and erected two buildings, which housed the University until 1871. After almost a century and a half as a teaching college, the University began to change with the times. Influenced by the German model of higher education, Penn transformed itself into a research institution, not only transmitting knowledge but now creating it as well.

Meanwhile, Philadelphia experienced its own renaissance. In the nineteenth century, manufacturing played a significant role in the economic growth of Philadelphia, and despite recurring financial panics and depressions, the city boomed between 1830 and 1860. By 1850, Philadelphia was the world's largest manufacturer of pharmaceutical chemicals. It was also a center for printing and publishing (as early as 1829, *Encyclopaedia Americana*, America's first encyclopedia, was published in the city), and there were active glass, furniture, and shipping industries as well.[2] After the Civil War, Philadelphia began a westward expansion, eased by the construction of great bridges across the Schuylkill River at Market, Chestnut, Walnut, and South streets. The University of Pennsylvania relocated from the center of the city across the Schuylkill River to the sprawling Almshouse farm. West Philadelphia was an area of wide open spaces, more verdant country village than big city.

Penn's West Philadelphia is reminiscent of the surroundings of many academic and health-care institutions in older cities, where growth and development in areas around the institutions followed similar patterns.

The prosperity of these cities was based on an earlier time, when the national economy flourished through its large manufacturing sector. Worldwide exports of goods from the United States came from these densely populated urban areas, where the manufacturing plants were located. Colleges, universities, hospitals, and research centers in these areas also grew and flourished, benefiting from the access to people, suppliers of products and services, and transportation systems. Many of these institutions developed their facilities in neighborhoods or unpopulated areas just outside the central business districts, further attracting housing and commercial development.

By the middle of the nineteenth century, West Philadelphia had a bustling commercial center, spurred on by the busy railroad station at 30th Street, which remains the hub of the city's railway system today. West Philadelphia was a community for the upwardly mobile, where mill managers lived comfortably in spacious three- and four-story twin houses. Their workers resided in smaller, more modest two-story row homes. With increasing industrialization, the area burgeoned. The opening of Presbyterian Hospital in 1872 created an urgent need for housing. Not long after that, rows of residences began to spring up as far west as 42nd Street. Some of the large estates farther out were sold to developers. West Philadelphia experienced a housing boom.

From 1850 to 1930, West Philadelphia evolved from farmland that provided a fashionable, upper-class country retreat to urban residential development. The advent of the trolley unleashed another wave of urbanization, expanding opportunities for employment and living, although not necessarily in the same place. Beyond the working-class neighborhoods of the city, especially West Philadelphia, Southwest Philadelphia, and upper North Philadelphia, lay a set of neighborhoods known as "streetcar suburbs," with streetcars providing easy access to the center of the city. During the late nineteenth century, most of the neighborhoods closest to the Penn campus were transformed into streetcar suburbs for working families (the West Philadelphia Streetcar Suburb Historic District was placed on the National Register of Historic Places in 1998).

This period in the late nineteenth century was preceded and followed by several decades of continuous growth for the city as a whole. The trolley lines that linked West Philadelphia to downtown ran (and still run) along three diagonal streets. Baltimore, Chester, and Woodland avenues were all developed during the late 1800s as neighborhood commercial corridors; a typical pattern emerged of rows of three-story buildings that had retail spaces on the ground floor and residential units above. In developing its new campus, Penn relished its urban location along an active transit corridor and knitted its buildings into the area's grid of streets. Students, faculty, and local citizens shared the sidewalks and patronized the burgeoning retail establishments.

By the end of the century, Penn was experiencing tremendous growth and construction, although it was still in its infancy in terms of what it would later become. The provost was the chief executive of the University: there was no president until 1923. In the 1899–1900 academic year, there were 2,673 Penn students. Fewer than 14 percent of them were women, and of those, nearly 70 percent were taking courses for teachers. The faculty numbered 260. Undergraduate tuition was $150 to $200 a year.

The University of Pennsylvania Museum of Archaeology and Anthropology opened as the Free Museum of Science and Art on December 28, 1899, on the west bank of the Schuylkill River. Symbolically, the museum was a bridge between the University and the city. The new law school building was dedicated in February 1900. The University purchased the "Foulke and Long property" between 33rd and 34th streets and bounded on the south by Locust Street for the princely sum of $112,500, adding several buildings to its holdings. That same month, the cornerstone was laid for the Memorial Tower and Gateway to honor Pennsylvania men who had served in the Spanish-American War. The tower, at 37th and Spruce streets, which still stands, was part of the University's new dormitories, which housed 350 students that first year and 525 the following year, when the tower and other buildings were completed. Still on the drawing board were a dining hall, a chapel, and additional dorm space to house a total of a thousand students. By 1913, the University had grown to 117 acres.

Early in the twentieth century, the first wrinkles began to mark the face of the streetcar suburbs as they grew less stable. The white-collar and professional workers with greater resources and earning power than other residents began to abandon these communities in search of new housing in the farther suburbs, leaving behind the less mobile factory workers. As people of means moved out of these communities, the larger homes and estates were sold off. Many houses became multifamily units, filled by transient workers and lower-income families. Many neighborhoods in West Philadelphia (as well as in North Philadelphia) experienced rapid racial transformation.[3] With less income to support retail establishments, businesses closed, leaving vacant storefronts.

By the 1920s, in one of the quirkier twists in Penn's history, a group of alumni who had complained about the neighborhood organized a scheme to move all or part of the campus to Valley Forge, miles from the city.[4] They were concerned that Penn had become something of a commuter school in a deteriorating area. The administration eventually laid the issue to rest as it became increasingly clear that Penn's future was inextricably linked with that of Philadelphia. Penn remained in the city and began to forge a partnership with a civic and political leadership that acknowledged the University's economic and educational clout and that facilitated campus development.

By 1930, Philadelphia was the third-largest metropolis in the United States. There were so many different kinds of factories in the city that it was known as the "workshop of the world."[5] Yet, as the years passed, there were periods of further decline in West Philadelphia, with attempts by resident associations and various private and public agencies, and eventually the city, to arrest the deteriorating conditions. All the while, Penn continued to grow. The Depression and World War II brought campus development to a halt, so it was not until after 1945 that the University really began to evolve into the institution it is today.

Immediately after the war, thanks to the G.I. Bill, college campuses were brimming with students. To compete with other schools, Penn had to expand. As early as 1948, its trustees approved a twenty-year master plan—one that emanated from national campus-design ideas of the mid-twentieth century—that would ultimately extend the campus west of 40th Street, aiming to make Penn a pedestrian-oriented "community of scholars residing in and around a campus closed off to vehicular traffic."[6] The notion of the university as a citadel of scholarly retreat was based on the European medieval ideals exemplified by Oxford and Cambridge of segregating communities of scholars from the outside world. Of course, the proposed expansion would require Penn to buy vast areas of land and the city to close several neighborhood streets. Over the next three decades, Penn would transform its environs in accordance with the plan, working with the city to turn as many campus-crossing streets as possible into pedestrian walkways. It would also embark on a series of multimillion-dollar construction projects orienting new buildings toward a newly formed commons, presenting a fortresslike appearance to passersby while providing the desired academic sanctuary for the faculty and students within.

How ironic that as, on the one hand, the neighborhood around the University began to implode in the middle of the twentieth century, Penn, on the other hand, was exploding. In the postwar economic boom, the government expanded its commitment to funding research and university-based training. With an enormous range of research grants available and highly specialized faculty competing for federal, state, and local grant money, Penn was becoming a major research university. Despite the neighborhood-unfriendly design policies that had closed off the campus to the community, Penn's administration was keenly conscious of the University's position as an urban institution, and its president at the time, Gaylord Harnwell (1953–1970), sought opportunities to define Penn's special role in the neighborhood and the city at large. For not only was the federal government expanding its role in funding scientific research, it was also beginning to invest in the improvement of America's cities.

The Federal Housing Act of 1954, like its predecessor urban-development legislation of 1949, sought to subsidize new housing and slum clearance, and encouraged public improvements of the neighborhood environment. New provisions required that each city receiving federal aid submit a plan for urban improvement. The Slum Clearance and Community Development and Redevelopment Program was renamed the Urban Renewal Administration. Now there was money for growth, but there were few models of healthy community development for urban universities to emulate.

Harnwell was not alone in his concern about the university's role in the city, as evidenced by an unusual 1957 meeting and ongoing communications among the presidents of MIT, the University of Chicago, Columbia, Harvard, Yale, and Penn that focused on how universities could ameliorate their respective urban neighborhoods. These institutions developed a number of strategies, including participation in urban-renewal programs that qualified for federal funding by the late 1950s.[7]

The prevailing theory among universities was that it was appropriate to use urban renewal to rebuild and control the neighborhoods, leaving "gown" dominating, or at the very least ignoring, the needs of the town. Rather than work with the community to rebuild and revitalize the neighborhood, universities typically asserted their muscle to restructure themselves without creating meaningful partnerships despite remaining marginally involved in the community. It is no wonder that town-gown relationships were often antagonistic; Penn's relationship with West Philadelphia was typical. With West Philadelphia on a downturn, the stage was being set for the next scene.

Over the next two decades, Penn and the city of Philadelphia rode the urban-renewal wave in tandem. Penn trustee Edward Hopkinson, Jr., chaired the City Planning Commission. In 1955, Penn's architecture dean Holmes Perkins succeeded Hopkinson as Commission chair. Penn trustee and alumnus Gustave Amsterdam, a real-estate developer, chaired the city's Redevelopment Authority for a time. When a huge apartment complex project planned for 33rd and Walnut streets by a private developer fell through, the Redevelopment Authority turned to Penn. Within a couple of days, the block belonged to Penn. And so it went.

With enrollment continuing to rise, Penn began to experience substantial growing pains, hemmed in as it was by heavily populated residential areas that left no room for expansion. Today, the vibrant area in which the University resides is known as University City. But until the late 1950s, "University City" as such did not exist. The area around the campus was simply a neighborhood. The name "University City" was essentially a marketing tool (probably coined by realtors) to attract faculty to move back into the neighborhoods surrounding Penn and other universities and colleges in the area (Figure 1). University City's creation as an entity was paradoxical—a response to the problems of West Philadelphia's decline and also the root of so many of the problems that Penn would face going forward.

In 1956, the murder of a Korean student foreshadowed the events that would bring renewed crisis decades later. After the murder, Penn and its neighbor, Drexel Institute of Technology (now Drexel University), took a hard look at what was perceived as the urban blight surrounding them and decided it was time to take a stand. In retrospect, it is clear that the focus was undoubtedly on the physical development of the area. New construction would provide desperately needed space for Penn, but it would also offer a more attractive sightline.

Plans were announced for the construction of Project "A," between 32nd and 34th streets and Chestnut and Walnut streets, the site acquired from the failed apartment project. Harnwell remarked that the project would reclaim a physically blighted area, and in subsequent comments his use of adjectives like "blighted" and "eyesore" echoed the language of city officials. To make room for the construction of what is now Hill College House, then a dormitory for women students, the blocks between 34th and Walnut and 34th and Chestnut would have to be cleared. The Philadelphia Redevelopment Authority sent appraisers through the neighborhood to work with local homeowners and smooth the way for demolition. Just about that time, commuting received a huge boost with the opening of the Pennsylvania Turnpike

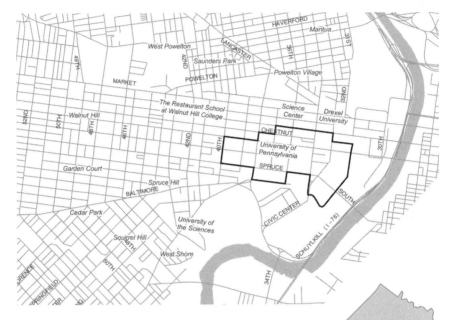

Figure 1
University City
Neighborhoods and
Institutions. (Inset)
City of Philadel-
phia map showing
University City
(outline) and Penn
(star). Adapted from
John Kromer and Lucy
Kerman, *West Philadelphia
Initiatives: A Case
Study in Urban
Revitalization*
(Philadelphia:
University of
Pennsylvania,
2004), p. 5.

in 1956 and the near completion of the Schuylkill Expressway, the highway that traversed the city and led to the growing suburbs. Although some residents faced with displacement initially balked, others came to view the University's expansion as an opportunity to take the money and run. The redevelopment process advanced fairly smoothly, but this incursion did not win friends for the University among those who chose to remain in the community.

As the 1960s progressed, major portions of West Philadelphia adjacent to Penn and other nearby institutions became part of the University City Urban Renewal Area. The Philadelphia Redevelopment Authority made this designation in order to support institutional expansion projects. It was using its authority to enable a strategy of land acquisition, relocation of residents and businesses, and clearance of existing structures. In return the city would benefit from construction of modern new buildings and enhanced growth and economic activity. In 1959, Penn and Drexel, along with other institutions in the area (the Philadelphia College of Pharmacy and Science, Presbyterian Hospital, and the Philadelphia College of Osteopathy) had formed the West Philadelphia Corporation, sharing the initial financial burden of the corporation, which would work in concert with public officials, interested citizens, and private groups, such as the Chamber of Commerce of West Philadelphia, to implement the "University City" concept as a first step in revitalizing West Philadelphia. The corporation would fight the creeping blight in the area by promoting development that would transform the neighborhood into an agreeable residential environment that could also fulfill its potential as a center of private education and research. An article in the *Philadelphia Inquirer* described Penn's vision, reporting on March 19, 1960, that "through its own building program and the West Philadelphia Corporation, the University hopes to create a 'university city' in its campus area by encouraging the sort of residential development that will attract its faculty members."[8] For Penn, this meant work at the eastern and western ends of the campus yielding new dormitories and academic buildings, many designed as so-called towers in the park (along the lines of Le Corbusier's mixed-use vertical city).

During Harnwell's presidency, Penn undertook the largest building campaign in the University's history up to that point. The University launched a massive private-donor fundraising initiative for a major expansion process, but the ambitious plans required government help as well. Local and state government augmented the federal grants in the overall expansion of the University, which took advantage of all of the new opportunities.

In October 1962, Harnwell and Provost David Goddard provided the trustees with details of a physical-development program, designed for completion by 1975, which would extend the campus westward to 40th Street and make it more self-contained and closed off. In order to implement the campaign, Penn would need to acquire city streets and more private homes for redevelopment. The University, a powerful force in the city, began using the redevelopment legislation to clear pockets near campus for current and future development, sending showers of disgruntlement through the local community. The core blocks targeted for redevelopment comprised 165 acres, three "urban renewal units" roughly bounded by Spruce Street on the south, 40th Street on the west, Powelton and Lancaster avenues on the north, and 34th and 32nd streets on the east (Figure 2).

The concept for the nation's first inner-city technology center was spawned from the West Philadelphia Corporation's vision of a centralized research center to complement the existing educational and medical institutions of West Philadelphia. Penn, together with twenty-four other interested institutions on the eastern seaboard, formed the University City Science Center to provide incubator space for emerging industries with the blessing of the city of Philadelphia, which anticipated nothing but good to come from such a prestigious organization in its midst. With Penn holding the lion's share of voting rights, West Philadelphia Corporation took the lead in winning federal funding to build the Science Center, a hundred-million-dollar urban-renewal project that ultimately demolished twenty blocks in

Figure 2

University City Urban Renewal Area, 1965. Penn's redevelopment
centered on Urban Renewal Unit lots 2, 3, and 4. Mackenzie
S. Carlson, "Come to Where the Knowledge Is:
A History of the University City Science Center"
(September 1999).

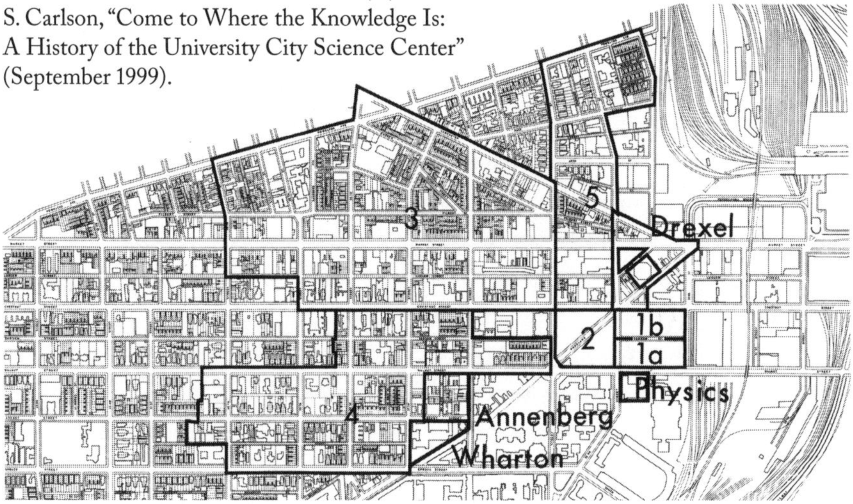

Black Bottom from 30th to 40th along Market Street and displaced
scores of families and merchants.

Understandably, the residents of this area did not sit silently as
they were subjected to what they felt were abuses of eminent domain.
Many were prepared to fight the destruction of their homes. For the
first time, student groups at Penn seemed to take an interest in the
situation just north of the University campus. There were demonstrations and protests. Lawrence Beck and Stephen Kerstetter, two
graduate students at the University, spent parts of the fall semester
in 1966 visiting the so-called slums of Urban Renewal Unit 3, inter-
viewing residents. Their findings were published in a five-part series
entitled "The Quiet War in West Philadelphia" that ran in January
1967 in the *Daily Pennsylvanian*, the University's student newspaper.
"The Quiet War," which was sympathetic to the displaced residents,
was notable not only because the *Daily Pennsylvanian* rarely featured
a series but also because the five articles were among the first in that
paper to discuss the redevelopment process that Penn had under-

taken. According to the series, Felton Newman, one of the area residents whom Beck and Kerstetter interviewed, claimed that "the West Philadelphia Corporation is a front for the University of Pennsylvania" and that Penn was "fostering segregation by moving all Negroes out of the area." The graduate students also found that other residents seconded the idea that "urban renewal means Negro removal."[9] Things did not look good for the University.

The 666 displaced residents who eventually found new homes with the help of the West Philadelphia Corporation were not all happy about what was going on. To be sure, some homeowners were glad to take fair-market value and move on, but the majority of the displaced were renters who wanted to stay put in a familiar neighborhood. And although the actual number of displacements belied the popular image of the Science Center as the redevelopment that displaced thousands of poor blacks in Urban Renewal Unit 3, the damage was done. The press had a field day, and Penn slipped several notches in the community's eyes. It did not end there.

In 1968, a group called the Volunteer Committee Resources Council surveyed four hundred people who had been displaced by redevelopment in University City Unit 3. In general, the survey suggested that while the majority of former residents were living in better housing, they were also paying higher rents. About half of the displaced persons considered the moving expenses they had received to be "inadequate," and 55 percent of former renters and 15 percent of former homeowners wanted to return to the neighborhood.

As for the University City Science Center, its development was anything but a public-relations coup. Intended to create jobs and lure high-tech businesses to the area, it did accomplish that to some extent, but overall it did not fulfill its promise. And its expressed secondary mission of combating community deterioration also failed terribly, because it did not provide many jobs to poor people in the area and did not ever integrate them into the growth process. By the time the building was completed, many in the community regarded Penn as the ravenous behemoth in their midst.

During the mid- to late 1960s, the University was mobilizing its resources to do what it believed would help cure urban ills, but others viewed it as protecting its own interests. By the late 1960s, Penn was heavily land-banking, buying up individual properties and clearing them for later use. One of the most controversial of these projects was the attempt to gain control of the row houses and Victorian mansions in a neighborhood called Hamilton Village. Twice delayed by community opposition, the plan was ultimately approved in May 1968.

When Penn began its huge westward expansion in an effort to "improve the neighborhood," most of Hamilton Village (including the townhouse where I had lived with fourteen other women as a student) was razed. The result was the so-called Super Block, a stretch of looming concrete high-rise dormitories (designed by a team of architects that included Louis I. Kahn, a Penn faculty member) and open spaces from 38th Street to 40th Street that displaced 1,220 people. It was reported that renters in condemned units were allocated $50 to $150 for moving expenses—hardly more than a token offer.[10]

While Penn engaged in aggressive urban renewal, Philadelphia, like many other cities, was continuing to experience a downturn. As the American economy became less reliant on its manufacturing base, the competitive position of older cities and their neighborhoods declined. Information and services now fueled the new economy, and these were based on technology and communications networks that were less dependent on location. Suburbs grew with the emergence of affordably priced, federally insured housing, and as these developing areas were linked to cities by modern transportation systems, businesses in newer and expanding industries began to locate in suburban office campuses and "edge city" office and retail centers. Shopping centers and suburban retail malls were constructed with shops conveniently co-located and ample parking, further enhancing the lure of the suburbs. All of these factors contributed to the population decrease in many urban neighborhoods.

White flight to the suburbs resulted in political and racial ramifications for urban neighborhoods. For example, after the middle of the

century, Philadelphia's population declined in every decade, dropping
from a peak of more than 2 million residents in 1950 to fewer than
1.6 million residents in 1990.[11] As the city's neighborhoods during this
period lost residents, most of whom were white, a weakened housing
market led to an increase in housing vacancy and residential abandonment in many parts of the city. As the population declined, there were
fewer people to purchase retail goods and services, and many of those
remaining were poor. Thanks to the proliferation of suburban shopping
centers and malls accessible by car, the loss of the middle class and the
reduced neighborhood buying power left holes in the inner-city commercial strips, increasing the number of vacant storefronts as businesses
stopped being viable. With the reduced tax base, city services and the
quality of public schools began to slide. Race relations worsened, and
pockets of urban poverty emerged and expanded. While businesses and
people in a position to do so fled West Philadelphia, Penn (like eds and
meds in most cities) stayed put, unable to lose the huge investment it
had made in its physical plant. Penn's campus had grown an average of
seventy acres every fifty years, and it was not about to relocate.

From the 1970s onward, the campus-planning and urban-renewal
programs lost momentum. Urban theorists like Jane Jacobs and
Herbert Gans, citing expense and dislocation problems, disavowed
the approach that such programs entailed. Large-scale redevelopment
programs fell out of favor at the national level as well, and in the early
1970s, the Nixon administration instituted a moratorium on all urban-
renewal programs while it sought a new approach, later devolving
authority to state and local governments through federally funded
block grants. Penn turned its interests elsewhere.

In 1970, following two decades of major campus expansion that
had removed a large number of homes and local businesses, University
President Harnwell began to rethink Penn's role and responsibility in
West Philadelphia. In an effort to mend fences with the community,
he created a new administrative position—assistant to the president
for external affairs—and appointed Francis M. Betts, III, his director
of planning and design, to the post. Betts's job was to try to develop

a response mechanism within the University that would put some of its intellectual talent to work on community problems, such as street crime, overcrowded schools, and job discrimination.

How was that mission translated into action? Use of University funds at the expense of existing academic programs was absolutely ruled out. Instead, Betts and his staff of two full-time assistants were charged with opening lines of communication between Penn and the community. They were to identify and resolve potential conflicts and grievances, while at the same time working with campus groups, committees, and individual faculty members to begin addressing the societal ills that were spreading rapidly through the neighborhood at Penn's doorstep. There were moderate successes and incremental gains, such as the creation of a presidential committee to address minority-hiring issues, and the establishment of a free school system that was a forerunner of today's charter schools. There is no question that Penn's institutional heart was willing and its mind was open to new ideas. But Penn also kept its expectations low and its pocketbook closed. As a result, unsustainable programs and initiatives like the Free School soon vanished, without a discernible positive impact on either the neighborhood or town-gown relations.

By the time Martin Meyerson, the urban-planning professor who had laid out Penn's plan for West Philadelphia in the mid-1950s, became president (1970–1981), the University was badly strapped for cash. Meyerson did not have the resources at his disposal to invest in the neighborhood. Crime was driving graduate and professional students out of West Philadelphia and across the Schuylkill River into Center City, and real-estate investors were turning dilapidated single-family homes into cheap group housing for undergraduates. Even Meyerson and his wife chose to live in Center City Philadelphia rather than in the immediate neighborhood. The mortgage program designed to attract Penn faculty and staff to West Philadelphia was extended to homes in Center City, sending a not-so-subtle message that West Philadelphia was not necessarily the neighborhood of choice.

The University reduced its growth aspirations but continued to seek available opportunities for expansion. One memorable and ultimately very significant battle was fought over the planned demolition of the 3400 blocks of Walnut and Sansom streets. Judy Wicks, long-time owner of the popular campus fixture the White Dog Café and a leading community activist, marshaled the fight against the university's encroachment. The Sansom Street Committee was comprised of professors and residents committed to retaining the quality of life that the street represented, with its mixed use of low-rise retail establishments and owner-occupied housing. There were all kinds of protests, petitions, and demonstrations. Eventually, the Sansom Street Committee sued the University in federal court. Hundreds of thousands of dollars were spent on both sides. In the end, the judge cut the baby in half: the University got Walnut Street and the community group got Sansom Street. But the animus remained.

Sheldon Hackney, who became Penn's president in 1981 (serving until 1993), resolved to improve relations with the surrounding neighborhoods. He recognized West Philadelphia's symptom of social disintegration and felt a strong commitment to the community and to the values of diversity and equality. In 1985, under Hackney, the West Philadelphia Corporation became the West Philadelphia Partnership, a name better suited to its new mission to become more inclusive in its composition. Its board of directors was expanded to include representatives from many more neighborhood organizations and institutions. Under the Partnership, there were campaigns for the University to buy more goods and services from West Philadelphia vendors and to hire more local residents, initiatives that were later expanded.

Penn also stepped up its outreach to the community. Hackney wanted a collaborative and participative program in which administrators, professors, and students could work with local institutions to do applied research on social and economic problems, enabling West Philadelphians and the University to solve some of those problems together. Ira Harkavy and Penn history professor Lee Benson spearheaded the effort to establish the structures and social processes that would make this collaboration possible.

Working with neighborhood leaders, the University established the West Philadelphia Improvement Corps (WEPIC) in 1985. Harkavy and Benson established a local base of activities in the Turner Middle School, the first step in developing a critical three-cornered relationship between the university, the school, and the neighborhood. Through the pioneering efforts of Harkavy, Penn led the revolution in academic-based service learning, in which faculty and students worked with neighborhood public-school teachers and students through the Penn Program for Public Service to develop rigorous, problem-solving courses that delivered tangible benefits to area school children.

In July 1992, Hackney created the Center for Community Partnerships (CCP) to involve alumni, faculty, and graduate and undergraduate students in working with WEPIC on the social, economic, and health problems of West Philadelphia. To emphasize its importance, he located the CCP in the Office of the President. He appointed Harkavy as CCP director. In many ways, Harkavy was the perfect choice to lead the center, having traveled a circular route since his student activist days at Penn in the 1960s, when he led protests against Penn's urban-demolition efforts in Black Bottom and its involvement with government contracts for the University City Science Center. Symbolically and practically, the creation of the CCP constituted a major change in Penn's relationship to West Philadelphia and the city.

The University as a corporate entity formally committed itself to finding ways to use its resources to help improve the quality of life in its local community, with respect not just to public schools but to economic and community development in general. Some of Penn's research and teaching would actively focus on solving universal problems as they manifested themselves locally in West Philadelphia and Philadelphia. By integrating general theory and concrete practice, Penn was getting back to its roots, doing exactly as Ben Franklin had advocated in the eighteenth century. The emphasis on "partnerships" in the CCP's name, like the earlier change from West Philadelphia

Corporation to West Philadelphia Partnership, was deliberate; it acknowledged that Penn would not and could not go it alone, as it had been accustomed to doing, often perceived as arrogantly so.

These programs succeeded in terms of breaking down some barriers between town and gown and opening channels of communication, but they failed to halt the decline of the neighborhood. They did not address the inherited problems of housing age and deterioration, as well as racial isolation and ethnic differentials in housing and economic opportunities. And without a sufficient job and tax base, it was not possible to alter the basic trends. Minus a large-scale commitment of money and resources, CCP alone was not able to stem the tide of further decline.

Further, there were still deep resentments in the community toward the University despite successful inroads at relationship building. Many residents felt ignored, disempowered, and in some cases harmed by an institution and powerful presence that they had come to distrust and fear. Penn's growth and expansion had effectively created a university island rather than an energetic, viable university city. Town and gown were far from functioning symbiotically.

By no means did West Philadelphia residents sit passively by. Community groups had begun to take action to protect their neighborhoods. Several groups drew up plans that served as seeds for the profound changes that would ultimately occur. One of the most vocal of these groups was made up of concerned Penn employees who lived in neighborhoods bordering the campus. In 1993, they formed Penn Faculty and Staff for Neighborhood Issues (PFSNI) and, after a year-long process of research, study, and discussion, released a report on action priorities for reducing crime, encouraging homeownership among faculty and staff, investing in retail amenities, promoting neighborhood economic development, and creating a viable public-school alternative within the local neighborhood. According to the report, "The fates of Penn and its surrounding communities are . . . inextricably intertwined: it is in the University's institutional self-interest to work towards neighborhood revitalization in both University City and, by

extension, West Philadelphia as a whole."[12] Clearly the elements of a
mandate, and an internal group of supportive constituents to be called
upon later, were developing.

The Center for Community Partnerships was also expanding its
role to engage in planning with the community. It worked with the
Spruce Hill Community Association's Community Development Task
Force to develop the Spruce Hill Community Renewal Plan. The plan,
like that of PFSNI, also welcomed Penn's involvement in reviving
University City and was created as a road map for the residents of "one
of America's first suburbs" to renew their neighborhood. It specified
residential and commercial strategies for five distinct planning areas
within Spruce Hill. In the plan, Spruce Hill was described effusively
as "a quintessential Philadelphia place that overflows with the greatest
American architecture and urban design of the late nineteenth century.
Its abundance of trees, shrubs, and flowers evokes lush cities of the
West Coast."[13] The plan was the 1996 Winner of the Pennsylvania
Planning Association's Top Award for "Comprehensive Planning by
a Small Community."

Following Al-Moez Alimohamed's murder in 1994, PFSNI addressed its concerns about the neighborhood in an open letter to me in
the September 8, 1994, issue of the *Almanac*, the Penn weekly publication. My response in a letter printed in the September 20, 1994, issue
read, "As I stated when I joined PFSNI's memorial walk on September
12, there is no higher priority for Penn than the safety of members of
the University community." And for two years we worked with these
groups and others who brought fresh, new approaches to the table.

And then the Vladimir Sled tragedy happened. The community
was stunned, frightened, and angry. Suddenly, there was a sense of
urgency about the revitalization of West Philadelphia that was unlike
anything we had experienced before. Or, as my chief of staff, Steve
Schutt, put it, "This was no longer a second or third or fourth priority.
It jumped to the top of the list and there was a sense of real institutional self-preservation at risk underneath it."[14] We were all feeling it.
Overnight, plans turned into action.

Fortunately, our leadership team had spent much of the previous year working closely with The Community Builders, Inc., a nonprofit consulting firm specializing in community development, and with local community groups. We had also been deeply engaging our own planning faculty. With them we had tried to learn from the successes and failures of other urban universities. We had worked to understand the best planning theory and practices in inner-city urban development. Based on these efforts, we had developed a vision, a strategy, and a plan for deploying leadership and resources. We were planning to act, and the Sled murder simply determined the start date.

We would strive to rebuild West Philadelphia's social and economic capacity by simultaneously and aggressively acting on five interrelated fronts. We would make the neighborhood clean and safe with a variety of new interventions. We would stabilize the housing market. We would spur economic development by directing university contracts and purchases to local businesses, many of which we would help to initiate. We would encourage retail development by attracting new shops, restaurants, and cultural venues that were neighborhood friendly. We would improve the public schools. We were committed to a spirit of seeking true partnership.

We also publicly vowed what we would not do. We would never again expand Penn's campus to the west or to the north into residential neighborhoods. We would only expand to our east, which was made up entirely of abandoned buildings and commercial real estate. We would not act unilaterally. Instead, we would candidly discuss with the community what we could do. We would not promise what we could not deliver. Instead, we would limit long-term commitments to promises we knew we could keep, and we would leverage our resources by stimulating major investments by the private sector. We intended to produce lasting results that would change the reality of living in the neighborhood and outsiders' perception of University City. Nothing short of a revolution would do.

CHAPTER 4

Policy, Organization, and Planning

WHEN PENN MADE neighborhood revitalization a top institutional priority, it committed to investing substantial institutional resources to improve neighborhood conditions and to focus on the root causes of deterioration. We understood that this required implementing intervention strategies to be carried out over a significant number of years. We were willing to leverage the University's resources, both intellectual and financial, and to lead a large-scale and long-range transformation of University City.

Commitment to deep and sustainable community revitalization required a series of policy decisions that together formed the basis for implementation plans. First, we developed polices to guide how we were to lead, administer, and finance the program of neighborhood initiatives. Second, we developed policies for how we were to undertake communication and coordination with other funding partners and stakeholders in the community. Then we developed policies to determine priorities for resource allocation.

Next we formulated explicit, detailed plans for all proposed activities, with an overall strategy for integration. In *Urban Development: The Logic of Making Plans*, Lewis Hopkins advocates that plans specifically identify decisions "that should be made in light of other concurrent or future decisions."[1] Careful to distinguish plans from governance and regulations, Hopkins notes that plans can serve various roles that are by no means exclusive. Plans can serve to mesh or reinforce agendas, policies, strategies, designs, and visions, and this kind of flexibility provides a structure for decision makers to match issues with solutions. Planning elicits discussion, argument, conflict, and resolution—all critical to guiding action. Planning also forces decisions about resource allocation.

Our plans called for extensive neighborhood reinvestment that would require a combination of capital, supportive services, and committed management, sustained over a period of years. This was made easier by the critical policy decision on where to locate responsibility for leadership and administration of the West Philadelphia Initiative.

Pat Clancy of The Community Builders, Inc., whose organization has spent thirty years supporting community-based organizations, surprisingly counseled us not to put our faith in the hands of community-based organizations, which "simply don't have enough infrastructure to assume that kind of far-reaching plan, particularly in the Philadelphia environment." Clancy said to us, "You need to have the confidence that what you are doing is in fact going to work and you can't have that confidence if you don't control it."[2]

His words resonated. We were also surprised and relieved to hear from many neighbors who welcomed Penn's involvement and leadership, provided we were prepared to make a serious commitment to embrace the neighborhood and operate transparently.

It boiled down to this: if Penn did not take the lead to revitalize the neighborhood, no one else would. Since we felt a tremendous sense of urgency, we chose to lead and administer the work. But in order to develop an effective, nimble leadership capacity, we had to reorient our administrative culture to work holistically toward simultaneously transforming the University and the neighborhood.

I recalled the words of William Zinsser, a remarkable writing teacher at Yale, when he spoke to a group of college presidents. He admonished us to recognize that timidity at the top is not becoming. If you're a president, be presidential. If you're a leader, lead. He said that nobody else can do it for you. Use your position and your gifts boldly. Take your stand—every day, if necessary—on the values that you believe in.

Beginning with the trustees and me, Penn's leadership would take full responsibility for directing and implementing the West Philadelphia Initiatives. With an initiative that would require such significant commitment of resources, it is no wonder that so many have asked (with valid skepticism, I suppose) what it took to enlist the support of the trustees. After all, the decision to participate in leading, managing, or allocating staff or funding resources to support a neighborhood initiative of this scale was especially challenging, as it would be for any urban institution. One can imagine the reaction to applying financial resources to a project of this magnitude when there are always so many deserving and compelling academic needs that are unfulfilled or underfunded. Certainly it did not hurt that Chairman of the Board Roy Vagelos, retired chairman and chief executive officer of Merck, had previously applied Merck resources and his personal leadership to Newark's redevelopment efforts. He became an early champion for Penn's leadership in the revitalization of the neighborhood. But more important, the facts spoke for themselves: crime was rampant, the public schools were failing, and housing prices were stagnant. It had become clear to the trustees that if Penn did not intercede, the community's problems would ultimately become the University's problems.

From the beginning, my senior leadership team and I worked closely with the trustees to develop and oversee the West Philadelphia Initiatives. The Initiatives were considered integral to the business of the University, and we embedded them in our first five-year strategic plan, "Agenda for Excellence (1994–1999)" and reiterated them in the second five-year strategic plan, "Building on Excellence (2000–2005)." And happily, I might add, when the trustees searched for my successor, they made commitment to the West Philadelphia Initiatives a criterion for selection. President Amy Gutmann began her administration in fall 2004 with stated support of the West Philadelphia Initiatives.

To provide for ongoing oversight as the Initiatives were implemented, the trustees formed a standing Committee on Neighborhood Initiatives equal in status to the board's existing committees on budget, development, and audit. A steering committee of senior Penn administrators reports to this committee three times a year. The formation of the trustees' committee and the reporting process underscored Penn's commitment to engage University leadership at the highest levels in the management and direction of the Initiatives.

Gilbert Casellas, an attorney and former head of U.S. Equal Employment Opportunity Commission (EEOC), became the first trustee chair of the Neighborhood Initiatives Committee. Not too long ago, reminiscing about the committee's role during the early stages, he remarked: "The strategy for the Initiatives was always a multi-pronged approach. We were addressing the University's role in the community. Our priority was to monitor the Initiatives appropriately. From 1997–2002, we really pushed. There was a good deal of collaboration in setting up an agenda. In retrospect, I thought then and I continue to see that it [the Initiatives] made sense. It was not a mistake. Other peer institutions don't usually do this at the trustee level but it was integral to the work of the University. Even after early reports of success, there was still lingering concern on the part of some trustees whether it was the right thing to do. But it has been a good investment."[3]

I chose to assign leadership, management, and communications responsibilities for the West Philadelphia Initiatives across all of the University's major administrative departments, as part of a broad, decentralized network that would link to our neighborhood and public and private partners. Overall leadership and direction for this priority was provided by the Office of the President through my direct participation and the assignment of my chief of staff and other senior staff members to handle key administrative responsibilities. Direction of the day-to-day implementation activities was handled by the executive vice president (EVP). The vice presidents of departments with major implementation roles reported to the EVP. A new position of vice president for government, community, and public affairs, reporting to me, managed ongoing communication and coordination responsibilities with government officials and community organizations. Despite the division of responsibility, there was constant communication—memos, phone calls, e-mails, formal and informal meetings—among all parties about the steps being taken in each of these discrete areas. It was essential that everyone was in the loop all the time (Figure 3).

The policy decision to place leadership, management, and communications responsibilities in senior University administrators is a key defining characteristic of Penn's approach to neighborhood revitalization and, in my view, positioned us for a greater probability of success in implementing the West Philadelphia Initiatives. Regardless of the elaborate policies and plans that had been developed, effective execution required a capacity for responding quickly to newly emerging issues and concerns as well as to unforeseen opportunities. We could manage the redevelopment activities with greater control and integration as an internal leadership team. We could also more readily facilitate access to investment capital, including that of our more traditional business partners (banks, contractors, service providers).

Additionally, the provost and the deans of Penn's twelve schools played a crucial part in the Initiatives. Official roles were assigned to the deans and leadership of the Graduate School of Education, the Center for Community Partnerships, and Penn Design. The goals regarding quality public education were implemented with the support of the Center and the Graduate School of Education. The Center coordinated campuswide academic resources to enrich new and existing public-school and community programs, while the Graduate School of Education played a key role in the development, organization, and operation of the Penn-assisted public school (described in Chapter 8). While the Initiatives were not part of an academic program and were not led primarily by faculty, we believed strongly that they had to be *academically informed*, with support for some activities provided by the University's Center for Community Partnerships and numerous academic programs. For example, the Department of City and Regional Planning undertook studio workshops on difficult develop-

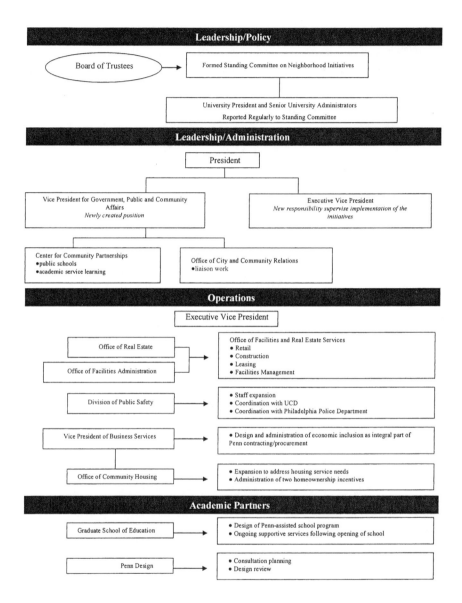

Figure 3

West Philadelphia Initiatives Delegation of Responsibilities.
Adapted from John Kromer and Lucy Kerman, *West Philadelphia Initiatives: A Case Study in Urban Revitalization* (Philadelphia: University of Pennsylvania, 2004), p. 12.

ment/planning issues, and the dean of Penn's school of design was deeply involved in all aspects of campus and revitalization planning.

Among the other key faculty resources used to support planning for the West Philadelphia Initiatives was the Neighborhood Information System (NIS), created by the University's Cartographic Modeling Laboratory (CML). CML, a joint venture between the University's School of Design and School of Social Work, brings together faculty members and students across disciplines to collaborate on urban and social-policy projects through the use of Geographic Information Systems and spatial research. CML's contribution was paramount in the planning process because it provided easy access to neighborhood-level market and demographic data, information that was essential to our real-estate staff.

In an organizational realignment that would prove to be critical, two University offices—Real Estate and Facilities Administration— were merged to form the Office of Facilities and Real Estate Services. This move enabled the University to consolidate all responsibilities for real-estate acquisition, development, maintenance, and management and to include campus properties as well as real estate acquired and developed off campus for sale or rental in the private real-estate market. Under one roof, we had architects, planners, facility managers, utility engineers, property managers, and development professionals.

The new vice president for facilities and real-estate services, Omar Blaik, took over from The Community Builders to provide "consulting" as well as coordination and implementation of much of the work. His focus was on integrating every element of the built environment across the five neighborhood Initiatives, linked to relevant campus planning and construction activities. The Initiatives had to find a physical form, in part, to communicate the transformation. In essence, changes in the physical space became a central element of the fabric on which the Initiatives were knitted together.

The vice president for business services, working with the Office of City and Community Relations, restructured and expanded Penn's acquisition services to make economic inclusion of neighborhood residents and businesses a fundamental part of the University's ongoing procurement of more than $650 million in goods and services. He was to assume responsibility for economic inclusion and make it happen, with key outcomes fostering economic growth and sustainability for the neighborhood. He was also responsible for building inclusion and opportunity into the homeownership programs. The University's Office of Community Housing, within the division of Business Services, was expanded to serve as an information and assistance resource for everyone interested in buying homes in West Philadelphia, and it administered the homeownership-incentive programs to encourage home buying in the area.

The Division of Public Safety not only expanded its staff and its security patrol but also worked in tandem with "safety ambassadors" employed by the University City District (a special-services district discussed in Chapter 5) and facilitated coordination of both staffs with patrol officers from the city's Police Department. It also developed a more robust community-policing framework and a more viable community presence.

It was clear from past experience in working with the various neighborhood constituencies that communication on all fronts was key to the overall success of the Initiatives. To improve opportunities for long-term collaboration (which was seen as crucial), University leadership established policies, as suggested above, for initiating and maintaining dialogue and information-sharing about the Initiatives with constituencies that needed to be involved during every stage of planning and implementation. Carol Scheman, the vice president for government, community, and public affairs, helped manage ongoing communication and coordination responsibilities with elected officials and community groups and other interested parties.

While we recognized early in the process that there would be relatively little city or commonwealth funding available, we involved local officials deeply in the review of all plans and were responsive to their questions and concerns. We communicated regularly with the mayor and with our local councilwoman, Jannie Blackwell, in whose district both the University and its West Philadelphia neighborhoods were located.

We worked closely, in particular, with the heads of Philadelphia's Planning and Licensing and Inspection Departments, who were critical partners. But all the city departments were supportive of and critical at one time or another to our efforts. We also met frequently with the state senators and representatives who represented our district as well as the governor and our two U.S. senators and House representatives.

Carol Scheman recalls, "We worked hard to ensure that our elected officials were involved in the early as possible stage. We talked about things they wanted to do and they had input in the process. For instance, on economic inclusion they sat at the table. They or their proxies were in every part of this aggregated work. . . . We tried to be very careful and clear about what we were doing and why and be responsible about it and be doing it for reasons that made sense for the overall mission of the University because that is who we worked for. I think we did a pretty good job and I think that made us a more reliable partner."[4]

Most important, we consulted regularly with community members and made certain that our leadership was not only visible but also accessible. For example, the University's Office of City and Community Relations instituted a monthly "First Thursday" meeting with representatives of neighborhood organizations and civic groups to provide information about current plans and activities, to hear ideas, and to respond to community concerns. The University administration also scheduled update meetings to provide information to and receive feedback from individual civic associations, nonprofit organizations, and neighborhood groups, and area-wide coalitions (such as the West Philadelphia Partnership), as well as with interested citywide organizations (such as the NAACP, the Urban League, and the Black Clergy of Philadelphia and Vicinity). And when there was more need for conversation with community-based stakeholders, Penn Praxis, a faculty-led consulting practice, played a critical role in facilitating the dialogue.

Obviously a great deal of effort went into public deliberation, and, like all public discourse, this was never smooth. Old grievances die hard, and Penn had earned a long list of enemies and suspicious observers. When a McDonald's sought to start a franchise in the neighborhood, a local group rallied against "McPenntrification." Although we had not recruited the McDonald's and shared in the community's concern, it took a long time for trust to develop. And, like the old joke, if gratitude and affection are what you want, get a dog. During my last year as president, in 2004, I was a guest on a local radio show talking about the West Philadelphia Initiatives and their success. When it came time for listener call-in, several callers aired their complaints and annoyances. This is not work for the thin-skinned.

Thus far, I have focused on consultation with all the relevant external constituencies. But faculty and students represented another key group of stakeholders and, not surprisingly, provided another group of critics and skeptics. And some of the concern was well taken. Should a university use its fungible resources on the kind of undertaking the Initiatives entailed? Would the Initiatives compete for new faculty positions, needed science buildings, classroom renovations, and student financial aid? And how would tradeoffs be debated and decided? These were the right questions. We spent considerable time addressing the issues with the elected Faculty Senate, the deans, and other faculty assemblies. And there were no easy answers. There would be tradeoffs, especially in the early period when we were able to attract few financial partners. We promised to raise new resources for academic needs (ultimately Penn raised $3.5 billion in new funds during the ten years I was president), but I was asking the faculty to trust me in the early days, to believe that a vastly improved neighborhood would benefit Penn academically, facilitate recruitment, and energize the campus. Many believed that it was the right thing to do and lent their support. But whenever we stumbled, as we were to do more than once, the critics came out in force. But so did the supporters, and, over time, pride in the outcomes and the visibility of real, tangible benefits won over many opponents.

Perhaps not surprisingly, our greatest supporters were parents and alumni. Worried that Penn's reputation was being tarnished by crime and deterioration in the neighborhood, alumni rallied behind these efforts. And parents, worried about the safety of their children, felt no amount of investment was too great. It did make me look forward to Homecoming and Family Weekends!

Our decision to "roll out" implementation of the Initiatives rather than announce a comprehensive master plan was informed in part by a sensitivity to all these various constituencies, a way of ensuring that each program was a collaboration between Penn, community members, interested faculty and students, and other supporters, and in part by a need to test and learn as we went along. In the matter of testing and learning, our view was based on the work of Charles Lindblom and James Scott, each of whom studied failed attempts at social change. In his 1990 book *Inquiry and Change: The Troubled Attempt to Understand and Shape Society,* Lindblom points out the impossibility of being truly comprehensive in urban planning from the start, because there are inevitable biases that frame the work in the abstract and there is an inexhaustible number of forces that enter into the life of cities over time that cannot be anticipated in advance.[5] Among the recommendations to social change that Scott advocates is to take small steps in an experimental approach, with the presumption that one cannot know the consequences of every intervention in advance.[6]

By launching the Initiatives as we did, we generated a greater degree of trust and active participation from within the community. We also made certain to provide opportunities for evaluating progress along the way and to consider ways of improving performance at three levels through (1) the Board of Trustees' standing Committee on Neighborhood Initiatives; (2) the executive vice president's supervision of University administrative departments engaged in implementation activities, reporting directly to the president; and (3) ongoing coordination and communication between University representatives and community constituencies.

Although Penn chose to lead and administer the West Philadelphia Initiatives through the University, this was not the only structural option. Every university ready to commit to and undertake significant urban development must seek to determine the leadership and administrative structure that best supports its goals. Several current models, in addition to Penn's, provide possible alternatives.

First is vesting responsibility in the public sector, for example a city development agency (the housing authority or the redevelopment authority). Such agencies may be willing to assume leadership and administrative responsibilities for revitalization of university-related neighborhoods. This does require, however, the agency's ability to administer multifaceted, multiyear revitalization efforts. Furthermore, it needs to commit to ongoing communication and collaboration with neighborhood interests to ensure that planned initiatives are broadly supported and produce maximum benefit for community members. Even if it does not assume a leadership role, government endorsement of an institution's commitment to neighborhood revitalization is essential. Its effective use of licensing, inspection, tax abatement and zoning, street cleaning and policing is a fundamental component of an overall intervention strategy.

A second option is leadership/administration by the private sector. It might be possible to recruit capable real-estate developers to handle property acquisition, development, and management responsibilities. However, while their expertise and partnership is crucial, it must be determined that the private developer has the capability or the mandate to lead and manage the type of multifaceted program needed to improve neighborhood conditions and stimulate a reversal of decades-old patterns of disinvestment.

Leadership/administration by an existing or newly created nonprofit organization is a third alternative that is sometimes considered in urban-revitalization projects. A model that relies on an existing not-for-profit entity usually has a local community development corporation (CDC) in the lead. These entities have neighborhood-oriented missions and are governed by community members. As a result, they frequently are willing to take on difficult, long-term projects in the interests of the communities they serve. Further, they often have ready access to government and foundation funding. Some CDCs, however, lack sufficient financial capacity to integrate a set of activities that include housing, retail establishments, economic development, and public education, or they lack sufficient organizational capacity reliably to lead and manage a complex, long-term reinvestment effort. As Peter Medoff and Holly Sklar point out, the problem is that in most neighborhoods where CDCs operate, new buildings go up, but for community residents the old obstacles to essential resources, jobs, and services remain.[7] Some of this is changing with the dramatic work of Local Initiatives Support Corporation (LISC) and Enterprise that supports CDCs in twenty-three cities through the outstanding "Living Cities" initiative.

Community-based development organizations can be crucial partners and allies for broad investment initiatives. If CDCs, for example, are experienced in sales or rental-housing development, they can play an important role in developing affordable housing. In West Philadelphia we were fortunate to work with two community-development corporations, the Partnership CDC and the People's Emergency Center CDC. Each was already working on an array of housing development and service activities that bolstered and complemented Penn's work.

Sometimes a new nonprofit development entity is created to lead the work, manage associated activities, and raise funds to support these activities from a variety of sources. A current example is the new 501(c)3 nonprofit that is successfully leading the redevelopment of East Baltimore with Johns Hopkins Medical Center, the Casey Foundation, and the city of Baltimore as the lead partners. The urgency of our problem made it less possible to wait to create a wholly new type of external organization to implement the West Philadelphia Initiatives. Furthermore, we concurred with the thinking of Douglas Henton, John Melville, and Kimberly Walesh in *Civic Revolutionaries: Igniting the Passion for Change in America's Communities*. They conclude that new networking vehicles rather than new organizations are more effective, creating the quickest and most enduring change, and actually help limit the natural opposition of existing organizations and their benefactors.[8] Channeling individual initiatives into collective action may yield better results by relying on networks that can be widely owned and are adaptable in design and implementation. They can initiate change more quickly and, if designed effectively, can demonstrate results in a relatively short amount of time.

Penn's administrative structure for leading and implementing the West Philadelphia Initiatives made sense for the University. It allowed for flexibility to act boldly, to avoid the "death by consensus" syndrome, and to sustain our vision over the many years that it would take to bring it to fruition. For institutions with fewer financial resources, this kind of committed leadership and structured coordination may be even more critical for success. It is not about the money. It is about the vision, the planning, the networking and communicating, the staying power, and the leadership.

By late 1996, we had a plan, a policy for leadership and administration, an evaluation mechanism, and the drive, energy, and enthusiasm of many supporters in the University, the community, and the city. We were ready to move ahead.

CHAPTER 5

Making the Neighborhood Clean and Safe

A CRIME WAVE on and around the Penn campus had been drawing national attention even before the murder of Vladimir Sled in the fall of 1996. The overall crime rate—from stolen bikes to holdups at gunpoint—had been rising since school began in September that year. This was occurring despite stepped-up patrols by both Penn and Philadelphia police, which resulted in an increased arrest rate that would normally contain crime. Then, in the early hours of the morning on September 25, a Penn senior was shot and wounded (but, thankfully, quickly recovered) in an attempted robbery while walking with two friends near 40th and Locust streets. This was a crime pattern that Penn's managing director of public safety, Tom Seamon, referred to as "unprecedented."

That night, Maureen Rush, director of police operations, spoke at a student rally outside Van Pelt Library, surrounded by members of the press. I knew that I also had to deal directly and visibly with this problem, so I called for an open meeting for 8 P.M. the next evening in the campus's Zellerbach Theater to announce eight new steps for increased security. It was a full house, and during the extensive question-and-answer period that followed, I was struck by some of the questions and ideas thrown out for consideration. It appeared that many in the audience were either unaware of or did not understand the safety measures we already had in place. Not only did we have to further augment security; we had to do a better job of informing our students and the public about what we had already been doing.

Part of the communications failure was due, I think, to a tension felt on most college campuses about policing and campus security. In kinder, gentler times, public safety was based on notions of campus policing that rarely included highly visible patrols, semi-automatic weapons in police holsters, video cameras, and investigative detectives. Students and faculty did not want to "feel" the police on their campus. Security installations like video cameras had no place in their free and open community of scholars. So we had stepped-up our safety efforts during the previous two years with minimal fanfare, seeking to operate without significantly greater visibility. Quietly we had retired the old timers and brought in experienced police officers, schooled in new, sophisticated techniques of city and community policing.

But now the situation had changed. The students and faculty were demanding more, and our efforts went public. We announced the increased efforts already under way and a plan to upgrade and expand security at an initial cost of more than $5 million. In addition to increasing patrols by Penn-hired security guards and city police, we installed security cameras on and off campus and a huge command center for monitoring these video installations. This time, I sent a letter to the parents of our students, assuring them that I understood their fears and outlining the plans to put them to rest.

A month later, Vladimir Sled was murdered. For weeks after the tragedy, John Fry, the executive vice president, was spending nearly 90 percent of his time on matters of public safety that had to be effected very quickly. Although the entire team was already involved to some degree in safety issues, Steve Schutt, my chief of staff, and Carol Scheman, vice president for government, community, and public affairs, were called on to handle the countless aspects of the crisis situation. Tensions were high, but this was a team of hard-driving individuals who worked well together, with the right balance of personalities, strengths, and weaknesses. Once we had a better grip on public safety, and as other initiatives that we were working on were rooted, we developed even more of an "ongoing strike-force structure," as Steve Schutt put it, one that we maintained to some considerable extent for the next few years. This kept the sense of urgency going in all our initiatives even though, fortunately, no more life-threatening tragedies occurred.

The "clean and safe initiative," laying out an intervention far broader than increased policing, had been in the planning stages for some time. Critical though police presence and security initiatives were, they were only part of what would make for a safer neighborhood. We fully subscribed to Jane Jacobs's "eyes on the street" thesis, which she described as, "The public peace—the sidewalk and street peace—of cities is not kept primarily by the police, necessary as the police are. It is kept primarily by an intricate, almost unconscious network of voluntary controls and standards among the people themselves, and enforced by the people themselves."[1] It was clear that in order to achieve safe streets, our goal had to be far more encompassing than an increase in police presence.

University City had succumbed to the broken-windows phenomenon, a premise spelled out by James Q. Wilson and George Kelling in a 1982 *Atlantic Monthly* article. "One unrepaired broken window is a signal that no one cares," they wrote, "and so breaking more windows costs nothing."[2] The theory suggests that evidence of decay, such as broken windows, graffiti, and litter, sends a message to passersby that no one really cares and, what's more, nobody's running the ship. In time, residents and workers experience an increasing sense of vulnerability and are less willing to get involved in maintaining public order or addressing the physical signs of deterioration. Absent a sense of law and order, the cycle stimulates a breeding ground for a criminal element that now senses that the vicinity is a less risky site for their activities. In other words, crime becomes contagious.

In his best seller *The Tipping Point,* Malcolm Gladwell writes that "the impetus to engage in a certain kind of behavior is not coming from a certain kind of person but from a feature of the environment."[3] If the environment was behind the growing crime in University City, then addressing the environment could prevent an epidemic. Despite the neighborhood's many positive characteristics—large, attractive older homes, parks, community facilities, excellent access to public transportation—the area's appeal was undermined by streets and sidewalks that had come to be perceived as dangerous or appeared to be poorly maintained. With a 15 percent rate of absentee homeowners and landlords, many homes and apartments had become rundown and seedy. The sidewalks were shadowed and seemed menacing at night. Few people walked after dark. It is no wonder that the area spelled opportunity to criminals.

University City residents were becoming discouraged. Barry Grossbach, community activist and longtime resident of the Spruce Hill neighborhood, recalled, "I was tired of wading through trash, and the general quality of life was no longer acceptable." But Grossbach had survived some tough times in University City, and he was loath to give up. He remembered, "When I moved there in the '70s, on 43rd St. off of Baltimore between Larchwood and Osage, it was considered a frontier."[4] But now Grossbach and other residents resented the trash and physical decay and worried about the crime—and these concerns soon overpowered the neighborhood's amenities. By the mid-1990s, University City had become as dangerous as it appeared.

We resolved to engage in efforts that would encourage the residents of University City ultimately to act of their own accord to enforce the public peace, as Jane Jacobs advocated. Increased policing was warranted and used more effectively than before. But we recognized that only by altering the physical and perceived environment would we begin to see lasting positive outcomes with respect to crime (Figure 4). It was up to Penn, as the largest stakeholder in the area, to step up as the agent of change. Working with the community,

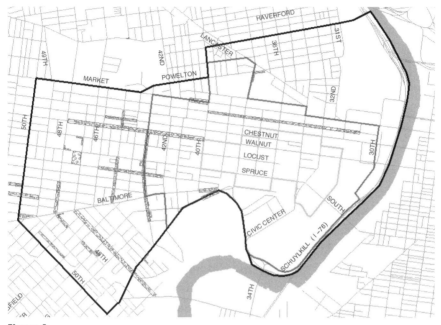

Figure 4

Policing, University City District, and UC Green Service Activity Areas. John Kromer and Lucy Kerman, *West Philadelphia Initiatives: A Case Study in Urban Revitalization* (Philadelphia: University of Pennsylvania, 2004), p. 21.

we would launch a campaign to repair broken windows, clean up graffiti and litter, light the streets, and, in Gladwell's words, "change the signals that invited crime in the first place."[5]

In November 1996, we launched the 40th Street Action Team, a nuts-and-bolts group of experts from across the University—in matters of real estate, police, housing, external relations, facilities— charged with the task of implementing short-term, marked improvements along the 40th Street corridor (a retail area in such decline that many perceived it as a no-man's land too full of foreboding to venture beyond). What made this work more compelling was that the team was charged to demonstrate an impact within forty-five days. It would carry out longer-term initiatives as well, working with neighborhood groups and merchants. But immediate progress had to be seen.

Cochaired by Maureen Rush and Diane-Louise (D-L) Wormley, then Penn's associate treasurer, the team was given a generous budget. What some team members considered even more valuable was the ready access they were given to John Fry, Penn's executive vice president, ordinarily so busy that "trying to get on his schedule took an act of Congress," as one member, accustomed to meeting with Fry at 6:15 A.M., put it.

The challenge for the 40th Street Action Team was to test which measures would work in the allotted time frame and which projects they could leverage over time—essentially a microcosm of our overall revitalization strategy, and a great way to evaluate ideas. The team concentrated its initial whirlwind efforts on 40th Street from Sansom Street to Spruce Street, a space of three commercial blocks. Resolving the most pressing problems was a practical matter, but each issue was viewed in the broader context of making the street look as though someone cared. What can we do to enhance this retail area? What would make the streets safer? How can we make the streets more inviting? The team studied the streetscape, then oversaw the repair of broken and cracked sidewalks and added bike racks and trashcans. When it became apparent that a power wash would not clean up the unsightly brown facade of the Hamilton Village Shops, the team painted the building a bright cream and installed colorful awnings. Team members wrestled with the city over the installation of pedestrian lighting until finally they got the go-ahead. Lights were ordered. New trees were planted. The team instituted weekend clean ups to get rid of the trash that littered the streets. They established a hotline for suggested improvements to the area. And when the Steppin' Out/Community Nite Holiday Celebration rolled around in mid-December, a tree-lighting ceremony celebrated and highlighted the first phase of improvements. Meeting the forty-five-day deadline was a commanding symbol of the University's determination to move speedily.

Next we attacked the issue of street lighting, which was so deficient that it was no wonder people were reluctant to walk outside once the sun had set. Penn and the West Philadelphia Partnership rolled out UC Brite, a measure designed to produce a dramatic and visible change. On a chilly December night in 1996, we announced the UC Brite program at an outdoor news conference on the newly relit 4100 block of Pine Street. I told the gathering, "It is our challenge to light every house from curb to door, from dusk to dawn. With this extensive residential lighting project, we are sending a strong message that we have organized to take the streets back." In instituting UC Brite I learned more than most laypeople need to know about energy efficiency, durability, and mounting levels. But far more important was what we learned about building effective partnerships.

UC Brite was a visibly successful example of public/private collaboration—Penn was allied with the West Philadelphia Partnership, who administered the program, and assistance was provided through Local 98 of the International Brotherhood of Electrical Workers and the Philadelphia Electric Company (PECO). Through UC Brite, we literally upped the wattage in West Philadelphia by adding outdoor lighting to city streets and sidewalks. UC Brite started with a $25,000 pilot program funded by Penn and four West Philadelphia landlords. The money was used to reimburse homeowners and rental-property owners for half the cost of purchasing and installing specified lighting at the sidewalk level, complementing the existing street and home outdoor lighting, in an effort to encourage safer pedestrian access.

The pilot program covered about 250 residences within the program's eligibility area, and the results were dramatic. Within the next eighteen months, UC Brite, led by its very able project manager, Esaul Sanchez, who worked through Carol Scheman's office, helped the neighborhood and the University install 2,500 fixtures on 1,200 properties. All the sidewalks were lit up with newly installed, very attractive post and wall lanterns, wall fixtures, and floodlights equipped with either a dusk-to-dawn photocell or a timer. The city agreed to trim trees around municipal street lights, which eliminated many of the foreboding shadows and provided better illumination. The lights brought a new sense of security and provided a far more pedestrian-friendly feel to the streets. By requiring all households on the block to commit to the program in order to receive the new lighting, we also encouraged a revival of block associations. I remember being invited to a block-association party, a gathering of new friends and old neighbors, to celebrate the success of "their" UC Brite block program. The neighbors had taken the program we instituted and run with it. UC Brite was very much a success story at a time when we really needed one.

By 1997, the University officially and publicly identified "safe, clean, and attractive streets and neighborhoods" as a priority. UC Brite was already lighting up the streets, and aside from the obvious benefits, it proved our first installment on building requisite social capital (Jane Jacobs and Robert Putnam each emphasize its importance in a well-functioning society).[6] Social capital refers to connections among individuals—social networks and the norms of reciprocity and trustworthiness that arise from them. Neighborhoods with high social capital are far less likely to decline in value than those with low social capital, regardless of other factors like racial composition, proximity to downtown, or residents' socioeconomic status. Not only did neighbors connect with each other through their experience with UC Brite, they also had convincing evidence that Penn was part of the fabric of their social commitment.

The streets were being lit up, block by block, but there was so much more to be done. Vandalism, graffiti, and poorly maintained sidewalks and public areas continued to convey the impression that the area was unsafe and rundown, no matter that the broken sidewalks were tree-lined and fronted some incredible architectural gems. To counter the deteriorating conditions, Penn took the lead in launching the creation of University City District (UCD), a special-services district modeled after Philadelphia's highly successful Center City District (CCD).

Jacobs observed that of city districts that yield real power, "Their value is rediscovered and demonstrated empirically over and over.

Not surprisingly, a reasonably effective district usually accrues to itself, with time, considerable political power."[7] Nowhere is this more evident than in downtown Philadelphia, where the Center City District transformed its area in the 1990s. In the preceding couple of decades, many businesses, discouraged by crime, homelessness, and lack of city services, turned their back on the city's central business district and fled to the suburbs. But in the 1990s, some of these companies began to lease office space in Center City and moved a portion of their workers back, lured in part by attractive financing offered by the city. There were other appealing forces, among them the work of CCD, which was a business-improvement district dedicated to keeping the downtown area clean, safe, and attractive. CCD was largely responsible for cleaning up graffiti, making the streets pedestrian-friendly, and actively promoting the downtown area by highlighting its improvements and competitive advantages. Special-services districts do not replace city services, but an effective organization works with the city and advocates improved city services. Today, CCD serves more than 2,100 property owners within its 120-block district, providing services that supplement both basic services provided by the city of Philadelphia and the responsibilities of property owners.

CCD was funded through a mandatory tax assessment levied on all tax-paying properties within the service area. This is the typical way such special services generate revenue. But this was not possible in University City, where a significant amount of property is institutional and tax-exempt and a property tax assessment would have not generated sufficient revenue to support programs. Nor did UCD organizers feel that property owners in the affected neighborhoods should be subjected to any property-tax increase. UCD was therefore established as an independent not-for-profit organization by eleven key institutions in University City and became the management entity for a 2.2-square-mile special-services district.

UCD encompasses several West Philadelphia neighborhoods that include 47,000 residents, 60,000 employees, and 40,000 students, making it the largest special-services district in the city, with the second-biggest budget. The organization's mission is to build "effective partnerships to maintain a clean and safe environment and to promote, plan, and advocate for University City's diverse urban community."[8] Today, UCD's programs improve streetscapes and parks, remove trash and graffiti, provide technical assistance to home and business owners, and increase public safety. Paul Steinke, UCD's first executive director and an energetic urbanist, hoped to emulate what Paul Levy, his former boss at the highly successful CCD, had done for downtown Philadelphia in terms of improving the physical environment as well as the public's perception of the area.

An earlier attempt to form a special-services district in University City had been launched but was, ultimately, unsustainable. Its story, however, is integral to appreciating its winning reincarnation. As I indicated earlier, by the early 1990s University City residents were growing weary of walking through trash and litter and becoming increasingly disgusted with the declining quality of life. Rather than turn his back on the community, Barry Grossbach threw his energy into the creation of an all-volunteer special-services district, pitching the project to anyone who would listen, including a few Penn administrators who served actively on a community committee.

Participation in the newly forming UCD was completely voluntary, and it managed to raise nearly a quarter of a million dollars in contributions from residents, businesses, landlords, and Penn. But the pilot program would operate for only six months—with such limited funding it was hardly a sustainable venture. In that short time, however, it proved that a viable organization could make a significant difference in the local quality of life.

By 1997, my senior management team was spending a great deal of time elbow-to-elbow with community leaders in meetings to discuss our mutual concerns. The pace was frenetic, and at times it felt as if we were in the midst of combat. Despite making inroads, Penn was still viewed by many as condescending and parsimonious when it came to investing money in the community. As we continued to meet with our community counterparts, worked on our problems in earnest, and talked to each other as colleagues and, more important, as friends, we began to dispel this notion. Together we debated how to harness the leadership and resources of the University to implement a sustainable special-services district. This time Penn was willing and ready to take the lead in bringing this initiative to fruition by supplying the lion's share of the funding, but we were mindful of the need for true partnership with the community and for wisely using the social capital that was accumulating.

Paul Steinke, then director of finance, administration, and business development for CCD, assisted with data collection and analysis as we tried to determine the boundaries and costs of a new district. Executive Vice President John Fry continued to be actively involved, attending meetings and crunching numbers. Tom Lussenhop, Penn's managing director of facilities and real-estate services, was serving as acting executive director and was the chief planner and point man for UCD, laying out the framework for the organization. Omar Blaik, then associate vice president for facilities management and a University City homeowner, was a tremendous supporter of the special-services district and offered his expertise freely.

Since membership in UCD, like the special-services pilot program that preceded it, would be voluntary. Penn agreed that its founding contribution would cover most of the projected operating budget for the first five years. Then we aggressively solicited every institution within the district, saying, "Look, we're not asking you to do anything more than what we're doing, but we're asking you to do something." One by one, other universities, medical centers, and several businesses signed on. John Fry recalls, "One of the most successful things we did to strike a good relationship with the community was to help form UCD. Yet, Penn took only a single vote although we could have opted for more since we were providing the largest percentage of the budget."[9]

In summer 1997, Paul Steinke was recruited to become UCD's first executive director. John Fry became chairman of the board. Steinke showed up for his first day of work on September 29, 1997, less than a year after Vladimir Sled's murder. When Steinke walked into his new office in Penn's Franklin Building, he saw a cubbylike, windowless space, which had most likely been designed as a janitorial closet. There was no computer, no paper, not even a pencil. I imagine Steinke wondered what he had gotten himself into.

The spartan office quarters belied the magnitude of the work that had been accomplished. Already in place was a fairly detailed plan about the organization's mission, along with the budget, and the organization and funding commitments were just about complete. Several local institutions had signed on for significant multiyear commitments, with Penn and University of Pennsylvania health system contributing what amounted to about two-thirds of the total annual budget, which began at $3.5 million and by 2005 had reached $5.7 million. A contract was in the works with the private subcontractor who would be responsible for managing the UCD security and public-safety program.

From the beginning of his tenure at UCD, Paul Steinke worked closely with Penn, meeting with John Fry almost weekly, relying on him for advice. Omar Blaik extended assistance as well as friendship, and the rapport between Steinke and Tom Lussenhop continued to develop. Steinke met regularly with the other member institutions and organizations as well. The joint group's esprit de corps fueled an almost zealous commitment to this first element of the community's revitalization. And Fry credits the coalition of people that worked together: "If you look around at what actually happened, it was much more than Penn, and people came from very, very strange places and came together and that's why a lot of good things got done. They deserve as much credit as we do."[10]

Just a month after Steinke's arrival, the first elements of UCD's safety and security programs were in place. Sidewalk cleaning and graffiti removal were being done seven days a week by twenty-four public-maintenance staff members who now clean about 160 square blocks daily, moving around briskly on attractive small rolling machines. Many of the earliest hires were welfare-to-work recipients from the local neighborhood. "Safety ambassadors" were put on the streets, their blue-and-gold uniforms creating a highly visible deterrent to crime. Nearby Drexel University made the first noncash donation (in addition to its annual contribution) to UCD by providing locker-room headquarters for the ambassadors.

Today, more than thirty-five safety ambassadors employed by UCD make an invaluable contribution to the well-being of University City. Equipped with two-way radios, these unarmed officers patrol the neighborhood streets on foot and on bicycles every day from 11 A.M. to 3 A.M. Each ambassador undergoes training in public safety and crime prevention, emergency first aid and CPR, interpersonal relations, and customer service. Ambassadors also track public hazards, such as potholes, problem street signs, blocked sewers, and broken fire hydrants, and their lists are forwarded to the city for corrective action. And because they are truly ambassadors to the public, each of them is schooled in University City and Philadelphia history, attractions, and services so that they can provide information and assistance.

Steinke's next move was to establish an independent identity for UCD by consolidating its programs under a single roof, out from under Penn's umbrella. And besides, he was understandably tired of working out of a broom closet. UCD moved into unused space in the University City Science Center. While this new office was still not ideal, it was better than the old one. And it gave UCD the space it needed to move the organization to the next level.

Once settled in his new quarters with several programs running smoothly, Steinke poured his energy into a marketing initiative dubbed "Go West—First Thursdays in University City," an adaptation of Philadelphia's popular First Friday campaign, which highlights the art scene in the Old City section. UCD hired a marketing and public-relations specialist and rolled out the campaign in the fall of 1998. The first event, an outdoor arts and restaurant festival at 36th and Sansom streets adjacent to the brand-new Sansom Common retail center, was wonderfully successful. Curious visitors came from downtown, and the neighborhood turned out. The event garnered terrific publicity, helping to spotlight the assets of University City and improve the public's image of the area. Subsequent First Thursdays included art openings, cultural institution special openings, screenings, performances, and other special events.

UCD's impact was unmistakable. The neighbors were seeing and experiencing the benefits of the special-services district, and so were we. In spring 1998, UCD hired Eric Goldstein to be its first director of capital improvements. Goldstein, energetic and creative, swiftly took on the role as advocate for Clark Park, the largest park in the community, serving some 35,000 residents in a five-block radius.

Encompassing 9.1 acres, Clark Park is a triangular oasis of green easily accessible by foot, automobile, trolley, or bicycle. All of us in University City recognized that Clark Park, with more than two hundred trees, was a diamond in the rough, a fabulous amenity that could pull together the neighborhood. Clark Park also had a fascinating history, thanks to its role during the Civil War. In 1861, the U.S. government started building a military hospital with 4,500 beds at the corner of Clark Park. After the battle of Gettysburg, tents for the wounded were set up on the grounds, and soldiers were transported there from a ferry landing at 42nd Street and the Schuylkill River. The Gettysburg Stone was placed in the park in 1916 to commemorate the 60,000 Union soldiers treated at Satterlee Hospital. The park is also the site of the Dickens and Little Nell statue, believed to be the only life-sized likeness of Charles Dickens, seated above one of his most beloved characters, Little Nell of *The Old Curiosity Shop*. The statue is itself a curiosity because its sculptor, Frank Elwell, was unaware of a restrictive clause in Dickens's will specifically directing that there be no monument or memorial erected in his honor, since he preferred to be remembered through his published works alone. After its exhibition at the 1893 Chicago World's Fair and then a controversial move to England, the sculpture was returned to languish in a Philadelphia warehouse. Eventually, the sculpture made its way to Clark Park, a treasure for the citizens of Philadelphia.

Clark Park had long been neglected and desperately needed to be revitalized. Trash and broken glass surrounded the Dickens statue and littered the park. More than once, the neighbors fought with the city just to get the grass cut. Lacking lights, the park was off-limits after dusk except to drug dealers and their prey. It was not the community gem it should have been, especially in a city so rich in parks. In fact, one of the joys of residing in Philadelphia is the fact that no resident lives more than a mile from one of the city's sixty-two neighborhood parks, all of which make up the 9,200-acre citywide park system known as Fairmount Park. However, the city was unable to keep up with the maintenance of so many public spaces. If Clark Park was to recover, it needed an influx of funds to update and maintain its facilities. Since its founding in 1973, the Friends of Clark Park, a volunteer citizen advocacy group, had been dedicated to improving the park. The community had its heart and soul in the park—it did not take much to recognize that a healthy, vibrant park could serve the needs of the neighborhood residents. Unfortunately, goodwill had not translated into cash.

Under Goldstein's leadership, UCD and the Friends of Clark Park initiated the Clark Park Renewal Project. Their first achievement was an agreement with the city of Philadelphia's Department of Recreation to hire a private contractor to supplement the city's maintenance of the park. The Friends decided that the only way to pay for the maintenance contractor was to hold a fundraiser, and they began to work with representatives from a number of the group's member organizations and institutions to plan the event. Jack Shannon, Penn's director of economic development, who lived in University City, poured his energy into the project, appealing for contributions from an untapped source—our many vendors. The weather for that first Party for the Park in May 2000 was as perfect as it had been for UCD's initial Go-West First Thursday event. The party was a huge success, bringing in more than $85,000 in corporate, foundation, and private donations, and it has become an annual fundraiser, with music, cocktails, and a modest amount of speechifying. Clark Park got its maintenance contractor.

Under the renewal effort, UCD, the Friends of Clark Park, and the Department of Recreation received a grant from the William Penn Foundation to develop a master plan to redesign and renovate Clark Park for the best possible use of the community. A steering committee, composed of neighbors, community and civic organizations, Penn officials, and political representatives, was formed to represent the broadest cross section of the community. The coalition solicited proposals from consultants for the development of the Clark Park Revitalization Plan, a community consensus on spatial organization of the park. The steering committee selected Simone Jaffe Collins Landscape Architecture, a woman-owned, nationally recognized landscape architecture and planning firm, to create the Clark Park Revitalization Plan because of its past involvement with similar projects, especially in Philadelphia. Working with Simone Jaffe Collins would be Eddie R. Battle Associates, Inc., a minority-owned business and consultant to nonprofit government agencies and community-based coalitions in West Philadelphia and throughout the Philadelphia region. Battle Associates would facilitate all meeting sessions and conduct interviews with key personnel.

Soon after, using the Clark Park Revitalization Plan as a guide, the city's Department of Recreation designated the two Clark Park playgrounds to be first on the list of suggested improvements. Clark Park's tots now play on new, safe equipment, thanks to more than a hundred neighbors, businesses, and foundations that helped to match a challenge grant from the William Penn Foundation.

Councilwoman Jannie Blackwell and the Department of Recreation committed $100,000 of city funds for renovations to the junior playground.

One of the most cherished additions to the life of Clark Park is the farmer's market. Every Thursday and Saturday from spring through fall, neighborhood residents and students, faculty, and staff from nearby universities flock to the market to buy fresh fruits, vegetables and herbs, homemade jellies and preserves, and a profusion of colorful flowers. The market has become so popular that it is now open during the winter once every two weeks, selling baked goods, jarred jellies and preserves, and root vegetables.

UCD's efforts in developing an enticing and vibrant urban area were creating a buzz. Things only got better when in 1999 Penn and UCD created LUCY (Loop through University City), one of our most visible and popular initiatives. This shuttle service was a welcome solution to transportation issues in the neighborhood and a great way to market the area. Although University City is well served by public transportation for travel to Center City and other neighborhoods, and Penn runs its own bus and shuttle service for students, faculty, and staff, none of these routes provides convenient, easy-to-use service within the immediate area. LUCY, named in a highly publicized contest, connects the transit hub at 30th Street Station to major employment centers as far west as 40th and Walnut streets and south to the Veterans Affairs Medical Center, alleviating the need for numerous institutions to run their own shuttles (often on the same routes). Consisting of six small, brightly colored, graphically designed buses, each with twenty-five to thirty seats, LUCY zips through University City, connecting commuter rail passengers and city transit riders alike to employment hubs. Students and employees of participating institutions (many of which, including Penn, contributed initial additional funding) and riders holding passes for SEPTA (the Southeastern Pennsylvania Transportation Authority, which operates the service) travel free; everyone else pays a special fifty-cent SEPTA fare. LUCY is a vital addition to University City, providing cheap, reliable transportation while reducing automobile pollution and congestion, not to mention freeing up parking meters.

With the introduction of LUCY, 1999 was somewhat of a banner year for UCD. The special-services district, which by then had outgrown its office space, consolidated its programs in a newly renovated building at 3940–42 Chestnut Street. The safety ambassadors are now housed in these quarters, and the Philadelphia police operate a neighborhood substation next door, allowing for a tighter watch over the community.

With UCD in full operation and working smoothly on a variety of fronts, we turned our attention to additional ventures that would make the neighborhoods in University City more attractive and increase curb appeal. The many vacant overgrown lots were eyesores that begged for attention. In 1998, UC Green was organized through Penn's Facilities and Real Estate Services, and Esaul Sanchez, who had directed the UC Brite program so expertly, became its first executive director. UC Green's mission was (and still is) to unite community organizations, city agencies, university students, and residents in local greening efforts. It was designated to be an urban gardening collective that would provide various types of resources and support, including design assistance, plant selection, professional contracting, tools, soil supplements, plants, and construction materials for neighborhood greening projects. These ranged from street tree planting to playground development.

UC Green, which recently obtained independent nonprofit status, works closely with Penn's landscape architects and has a strong community advisory board, with student representation from local universities and high schools. It collaborated with the Pennsylvania Horticultural Society and the Philadelphia Fairmount Park Commission to survey all existing street trees in University City, mitigate any observed problems, and lead extensive new tree-planting efforts. It engages in several streetscape improvement projects and leads home gardening and landscaping projects. The energy and dedication of UC Green is remarkable. Stroll through the area on a weekend in the fall or spring and one is likely to find neighborhood groups and student volunteers from Penn, as well as other colleges and high schools, clearing debris, hauling, and planting lawns for homes and public spaces. Organizations like UC Green accomplish much more than their primary mission. They provide a way for people from different backgrounds to work together, an especially effective way to strengthen the social fabric of a community. More and more social capital was accumulating.

As we continued to work on these environment-improvement efforts, safety and security were still very much on our minds. We had made strides in these areas but recognized the need to continue to invest heavily in Penn's own public-safety division. Again we hired more officers. We focused especially on increasing the number of police bicycle patrols, which put officers in closer contact with the community and increased the speed with which they patrolled. We developed a highly sophisticated investigative unit. We established a new level of cooperation with the Eighteenth District of the Philadelphia police, which enabled us to access and coordinate an increased number of foot patrols and tactical squads. Our own University police force patrolled further out into the community. We created the position of director of security systems for deploying new campus and community security technology.

We were doing a great deal more to make our campus safer and to integrate the needs of the community with our own. The various neighborhoods of University City had their own active Town Watch organizations, and we met with representatives from several of those groups along with city officials to enhance neighborhood watch efforts. We established a much greater security and public-safety presence and visibility in the neighborhood, and through these efforts we began to chip away at the town-gown barricades.

Clean and Safe Initiative Results

PUBLIC SAFETY

❖ Crime reports requiring a response by the Division of Public Safety dropped by 40 percent overall between 1996 and 2002, with a 56 percent reduction in robberies, a 28 percent reduction in assaults, a 31 percent reduction in burglaries, and a 76 percent reduction in auto theft.

❖ Crime dropped an additional 14 percent overall between 2002 and 2003.

❖ In a 2001 survey of community members, 70 percent of the respondents indicated that the neighborhood's atmosphere had improved dramatically, and 71 percent indicated that they felt very safe in University City.

❖ Security on Campus, a national nonprofit organization, awarded Penn's Division of Public Safety the 2003 Clery Award, in recognition of the division's "innovative technological programs as well as its campus and community patrols."

OTHER NEIGHBORHOOD SERVICES

❖ Each year, UCD staff remove more than 2,500 graffiti "tags" and more than a million pounds of trash from the area.

❖ More than 150,000 copies of the UCD-published *University City Visitors Guide* have been distributed throughout the region, and the UCD Web site is visited more than 20,000 times monthly.

❖ In 2002, UCD raised more than $350,000 for programs to assist small businesses throughout the area. With support provided through UCD's commercial-corridor program, eight new stores opened.

❖ Since 1997, UCD has leveraged more than $5 million to support signage, landscaping, transportation, and public open-space improvements in University City.

❖ The UC Brite program has brought more than 2,500 lights to almost 1,400 properties since 1996.

❖ UC Green renewed more than twenty-five residential blocks, created three children's gardens and five public gardens, and planted a thousand spring bulbs throughout the neighborhood.

❖ UC Green has planted more than 450 street trees on residential and main streets throughout University City, mobilizing more than 1,200 volunteers.

Source: John Kromer and Lucy Kerman, *West Philadelphia Initiatives: A Case Study in Urban Revitalization* (Philadelphia: University of Pennsylvania, 2004), p. 24.

And because public safety, with its increasing complexities and re-sponsibilities, called for a more professional setting, Penn also invested in a new home for its Division of Public Safety. In 1999, Public Safety moved off campus and into a new headquarters building strategically located in the community at 4040 Chestnut Street, just down the block from UCD and the Philadelphia police substation. The new address was symbolic, because it said to the community, "We're here to watch over the neighborhood as well as the campus." And to the criminal element, these same words served as a warning. Such close proximity between the public-safety and security staffs of Penn, city police officers, and UCD on the next block allowed for the kind of cooperation and collaboration that benefited public safety throughout the district.

In 2000, the Department of Public Safety merged the UCD Safety Ambassador Program into Penn's security patrol, which enabled the boundaries and hours of operation to be extended even further. The campus-safety leaders of all the area colleges and universities began to work together to coordinate their efforts. The Department of Public Safety also became more active in the community by holding safety education programs and rape aggression defense clinics, and by hosting a local police athletic league program for neighborhood kids. Public Safety also created a community-relations-officer position to address the issues and concerns of neighborhood organizations and civic associations.

The results of these efforts are reflected in crime statistics, streetscape improvements, neighborhood perception, and awards. John Kromer and Lucy Kerman's analysis (see box) shows evidence of marked success. We had come a long way in a short time. Penn's presence as a commu-nity leader was being recognized. We had demonstrated, by our level of personal and financial contributions, that we were committed to revitalizing University City. But we were just warming up—there was so much more to do, and we were in it for the long haul. That meant continuing to move in a number of interdependent areas, including the critical issue of housing. Unless the declining and deteriorating housing market in University City was stabilized, the community could not thrive. We believed that Penn had the resources, the creative talent, and the drive to help turn the housing market around. We were challenged by many naysayers. We made it our mission to prove them wrong.

CHAPTER 6

Reclaiming Housing

As I went back and forth on the stretch of Walnut Street between my home (the president's house, known as Eisenlohr Hall) and my office in College Hall during my final years as president, I never failed to be thrilled by the energy and excitement of the area. Where parking lots and barren parcels of land had once dominated, pedestrians now strolled past thriving shops and an eclectic mix of restaurants that catered to an equally diverse mix of customers. The streets and sidewalks were clean, free of litter. And the houses and apartments looked refreshed and inviting. Most important, they were now lived in. It was a far cry from when I arrived in 1994. Then, many of our own faculty members and administrators actually steered new prospects away from buying in University City, despite the charming and inexpensive housing stock.

We knew we had to intervene to make buying a home in University City more attractive. In spite of its shortcomings, the neighborhood had much to offer with its unique character that could be tremendously appealing. In most urban neighborhoods, home ownership forms the backbone of community stability. The level of occupant-ownership in University City has traditionally been significantly lower than in the city of Philadelphia as a whole. In 1990, University City had an owner-occupancy rate of 22 percent, compared to the city's overall rate of 62 percent.[1] No doubt University City neighborhoods, like those surrounding all urban eds and meds, will always have a significant demand for rental housing. Undergraduate student renters are transient, often moving from year to year, and while graduate students, postdocs, and interns stay somewhat longer, they rarely commit to purchasing homes. University neighborhoods are inevitably subject to population turnover and residential instability. Consequently, it is essential to recruit and retain homeowners, who are typically stable, long-term residents. They have more investment in the community, literally, and although they are not always better citizens than renters, they do represent much-needed stability and balance. Homeowners' decisions regarding whether to improve their properties, maintain their properties, or allow them to decline depends on a combination of household characteristics, property characteristics, and neighborhood characteristics.[2] Yet, a homeowner's ultimate *incentive* to invest stems from the neighborhood, and expectations about its future quality and value.[3]

In the previous two and a half decades, Penn affiliates accounted for only about one-quarter of the housing sales in University City each year, numbers that belied the fact that Penn was the largest private employer in the city. A thirty-year-old mortgage-guarantee program offered by the University was satisfactory, but it was never marketed properly and was not specifically designed to attract Penn affiliates to, and keep them in, West Philadelphia. Instead, the target area included the western portion of Center City, across the Schuylkill River. The mortgage program did not benefit Penn faculty and staff already living in West Philadelphia, some of whom could have used help in financing the repair and improvement of the older houses they owned. With only one lender serving the program, qualified employees could usually secure better rates elsewhere, and they did. There simply were not enough incentives for Penn affiliates seeking to buy homes. As a result, only a handful of employees used the mortgage program each year, and of those who did, many bought homes in Center City. We could do much better.

But a weak mortgage program was not the most vexing problem. By the mid-1990s, the local real-estate market had been stalled by a combination of forces. Homeowners were fleeing, and in the University

City rental market, absentee landlords with multiple properties found themselves caught in a downward spiral. Many were fully leveraged, unable to make mortgage payments as rents plummeted. Lacking sufficient income to make repairs, landlords let the properties deteriorate. There was enormous fallout in the multifamily and single-family housing markets as more and more owner occupants left the area. When they were not able to sell their properties for the prices they wanted, homeowners put in tenants—any tenants—as long as they could pay the rent.

Kate Ward Gaus, Penn's associate director for health education, has known the community for most of her life. Until Gaus was school age, she lived with her family in her grandparents' three-story twin house at 43rd and Pine streets. When her parents bought their own home, the family moved to 65th Street and Chester Avenue in Southwest Philadelphia. During college, Gaus and her friends rented in West Philadelphia. And in 1978, she and her husband bought their first house, at 48th and Pine streets, where they still live today.

"We were all buying what we thought were affordable starter homes, as long as we were willing to put in sweat equity," she recalls.

> Most of my friends in other parts of Philadelphia were paying forty thousand for a house, but we paid only twenty-four thousand dollars. There are no words to describe what a fixer-upper this house was—a triplex in appalling condition. Two of the units were occupied by young single moms with small children. The heat was barely working and the pipes didn't work. But the three-story twin was eighteen feet wide, seventy-five feet deep, and another twenty-five feet deep when you count the yard. Most of the homeowners on the block were in their fifties and sixties, solid middle-class families who had already raised children who fled the neighborhood. We were the young upstarts. The impression we got from our neighbors was that the 1970s had been difficult in terms of many of their neighbors

moving out and others renting out their houses or selling to developers or people who weren't invested in keeping them up. But from the point when we bought until the mid-eighties, it was quite dynamic. Among the older homeowners, there was this level of "Oh wow, there's some new energy here." They liked the idea of the houses being bought by people who were going to live in them. We were fixing up our homes, having children, and getting involved in community associations.[4]

Despite this enthusiasm, the 1980s were marked by a 12 percent decline in overall owner-occupied housing in West Philadelphia. Many of the houses suffered from neglect—or worse, abandonment. As formerly satisfactory properties deteriorated, they attracted a lower caliber of tenant. And when crack cocaine hit the neighborhood, it brought with it increasing crime. Kate Ward Gaus remembers multiple break-ins, one of which occurred in the kitchen while she was sitting unaware on the front porch. People began to move out of the area, but others, like Gaus and her husband, were resolute about staying. They continued to pour their energies into the homes in which they had invested so much time, labor, and love and into the neighborhoods that they had worked so hard to sustain and improve.

By 1989, the local real-estate bubble, mimicking the national market, had burst. Efforts increased to lure homebuyers to the area, especially as mortgage rates became more attractive. In 1991, the all-volunteer University City Promotions Group devised a clever plan to address the exodus of owner-occupants and the resulting rise in tenant residency. They created University City Saturday Community Open House, based on the concept that realtors do not sell houses, neighbors do. Every house on the market was open on that one day, hosted by a neighbor rather than a real-estate agent. The kick-off was at a local church. In this way, a newcomer considering settling in the neighborhood could meet with representatives of organizations committed to the area and learn exactly what the community had to offer. Realtors, lenders, and community associations were available to answer questions. The event allowed a busy couple with kids, who ordinarily might at best be able to look at a few houses on a Tuesday night and a few more over the weekend, an opportunity to breeze through twenty properties in a single day. Although this way they saw only a fraction of the listings, it gave them a chance to experience the flavor of the architecture, the neighborhood, and the people. The neighbor who staffed the open house would point out the advantages of living there—great block parties, lots of kids, a sense of community—and share his or her own experience as a resident. So successful was University City Saturday that the idea has been copied in other cities.

Even with the triumph of University City Saturday, however, a large stock of houses remained for sale, and for those homes, actual days on the market stretched out. Penn sociology professor Dennis Culhane was a University City resident who remained in the neighborhood and took advantage of what he refers to as the housing "white sale" of the early to mid-1990s. In 1990, Culhane and his wife bought their first house. Just a little more than five years later, they bought another. Realty listings in the area at that time were so plentiful that they filled a double-sided legal-sized sheet with two columns on each page. The Culhanes purchased a five-thousand-square-foot home with seven bedrooms and four baths on three floors, and a two-car garage with a private alley. The house had been on the market for six months, and the Culhanes paid $70,000 less than the asking price.

Like the Gaus and Culhane families, many Penn affiliates enjoyed the advantages of University City living. The close proximity to campus (most people walked to work) and to the cultural attractions of nearby Center City was a real benefit. The local swimming club was a terrific gathering place in the summer, and a sense of community prevailed. But as the years passed, social life too often became a round of farewell parties as friends whose children had reached school age fled to the suburbs. Many cited the necessity to avoid private-school tuition as the main factor in relocating. Culhane, however, contends that the growing perception that the neighborhood was no longer safe fueled much of the migration, since these same people who moved out sent their children to private schools anyway, despite living elsewhere.

The housing situation in University City had clearly reached a tipping point, and Penn's time to intervene had arrived. In planning the housing initiatives, we sought solutions that would rebuild capacity into the neighborhood, that would stimulate the local real-estate market and encourage revival of a real and substantially diverse community. A mountain of data drove the planning for the housing initiatives. We used census data, municipal records, real-estate-market data, and other data from GIS mapping to evaluate the neighborhood development potential block by block and to identify, implement, and monitor institutional actions designed to take advantage of available opportunities. And for every option considered, we applied a litmus test: Would it promote systemic change and also allow the community to remain economically and racially diverse? Analysis of other university-led efforts had demonstrated how the unintentional forces of upward mobility and the transmigration of populations from one neighborhood to another can destroy ethnically, racially, and economically mixed communities. These efforts often wiped out the character of a community by failing to provide the mix of housing options that sustain a diverse neighborhood.

The plan for the housing initiative was to provide a broad spectrum of housing choices for owners and renters. The potential already existed in University City, but the available options required substantial rehabilitation and modification. There were many blocks in which well-kept homes were devalued by one dilapidated or abandoned house in their midst, harbingers of the vicious cycle predicted by the broken-windows theory. Of the numerous multifamily buildings in the area, many were neglected and badly managed by indifferent or financially strapped landlords. And as the housing stock deteriorated, more and more single-family homes were rented out, increasingly to undergraduates.

Potential homebuyers were not anxious to buy a house next door to one that was occupied by a group of students. Penn undergrads, like undergrads anywhere, can be loud, boisterous, and messy—taking out the trash is just not a priority for a twenty-year-old, and parties lasting till 2 A.M. were routine. In fact, this was another reason to bring our undergraduate students back to on-campus living, a goal already designated as one of our highest academic priorities. It is important to note that a university can affect the neighborhood housing market dramatically simply by changing its own on-campus housing policies and practices, such as the number of available on-campus beds for undergraduates, the quality of the on-campus residential experience, and whether or not students are required to live in campus housing if it is available.

Improving the undergraduate campus residential experience became a huge leverage point in our neighborhood strategy. In 1998, we began a concerted effort to improve on-campus living by introducing the College House System, which transformed all of Penn's residential facilities into college houses that fostered a greater intellectual community and provided essential advising and support for academic and cocurricular activities. This fulfilled academic goals articulated by the faculty and brought more undergraduates out of West Philadelphia, freeing multifamily units to be returned to the market for single-family purchase. Other interventions to prime the owner-occupied housing market were introduced in successive cycles over time.

Penn's multifaceted housing strategy for West Philadelphia was designed to target each of the problem areas associated with poor-quality housing. In partnership with city agencies and community groups, we would acquire, improve, and recycle deteriorated or vacated properties in key locations. We would work actively with the Philadelphia Licensing and Inspection Department on code enforcement. We would offer excellent homeownership and home-improvement incentive programs. We would improve the availability, affordability, and quality of rental housing in University City.

We were, basically, committing to turning around a real-estate market. Penn's trustees shared our conviction that the housing initiative was an imperative if the neighborhood was to survive, and they became investors. They demonstrated their trust in our team by allocating $2 million for the initial housing initiative—rehabilitating vacant housing.

It was our money to use, and lose, on what was called the Vacant House Rehabilitation Program.

So began our entrée into the rehab business in an effort to stabilize the neighborhood and stimulate new investment in West Philadelphia real estate by taking on abandoned properties. Applying the following litmus test, we asked, "If we fix an abandoned house on a block, will it protect the other houses on that block?" We understood that "gap toothing," the practice of leaving an empty lot after tearing down a twin or row home, not only weakens the structure of the remaining houses but is also a surefire way to diminish the value of a block. Why would anyone want to buy a house on a street with an abandoned lot or a decrepit house if other options were available? With this program, we were buying and rehabilitating abandoned properties to resell them, often at a loss, to help turn around the community.

Despite the fact that Philadelphia has more vacant lots and abandoned buildings per capita—36.5 per thousand residents—than any other city in the nation, identifying these properties was no easy job. Sometimes it is difficult to discern when a property is in the process of becoming abandoned or is definitively abandoned. Using data from Dennis Culhane's cartographic modeling lab and consulting with local residents, Pat Clancy from The Community Builders, Inc., and Lindsay Johnson of Common Ground Realtors identified those streets where abandoned or dilapidated housing threatened the viability of the block. Twenty vacant houses in strategic spots throughout the University's designated homeownership target area were acquired for rehabilitation and resale as owner-occupied homes.

Just because a house was identified for rehabbing did not mean its acquisition was assured. For example, on one block stood a house in such deplorable condition that it probably should have been condemned. But instead, twenty people were living in it. The house had belonged to an elderly owner, and the estate was tied up in probate. With the immediate family living out of town, the vacant house had been taken over by other family members. Other similarly abandoned houses invited squatters. Abandoned houses came with a history or, as realtor Lindsay

Johnson liked to say, "Dilapidated houses come with dysfunctional families." Those were the kinds of properties that prospective home-buyers avoided, the same kind that threatened to bring down the whole block with them.

With help from local councilwoman Jannie Blackwell, we negotiated with the city to forgive some of the liens and back taxes on several of these properties. The city recognized that we were not going to make a profit from these acquisitions and that our investment would ultimately benefit Philadelphia. No private investor was going to spend $100,000 for a house that needed at least another $100,000 for renovation, when the absolute top of the market was $125,000. Penn was the only player willing to step in, and we were purchasing houses that no one else would touch. In this approach, the University served as both housing developer and source of housing subsidy.

We won some and we lost some. The city had already removed the porch and the bay window of a house, in preparation for leveling it, when we got involved and saved it from demolition. In the case of a property that we did not yet own, we had to authorize someone to go in and fumigate it before we could even get a contractor to look at it. For five years, the house had been a haven for numerous neighborhood cats that scampered in and out through the open windows. We even bought a burnt-out shell. One particularly painful loss was a potentially magnificent four-story Victorian house in such bad shape that it was condemned by the city. It was razed (despite protests from preserva-tionists and community members) before we could intervene. And the legal headaches were incredible. Obtaining clear titles for many of the properties was often a bureaucratic nightmare and took months of legal wrangling.

But our involvement began to have a ripple effect. Once work started on these houses and the subcontractors began swinging hammers, the enthusiasm was contagious. As a block was improved by the rehabbed property, there was a noticeably renewed sense of pride. Homeowners began the painstaking restoration of the intricate gingerbread trim on their Victorian homes. They painted the exteriors and landscaped.

The degree to which renovation stimulated further investment can be seen in the case of a vacant three-story house on the 4200 block of Pine Street. The University spent $240,000 to acquire and rehab this house, which we sold for $200,000, spending $40,000 in subsidy expense from the $2 million fund of resources that the trustees had allocated. But the investment was well worthwhile. Within three years of the Pine Street sale, nearly half of the other houses on the block had been repainted and spiffed up. Several homeowners transformed the paved concrete areas in front of their homes into landscaped yards with grass and plantings. Trees were planted on both sides of the street. Certainly, not all of these changes can be directly attributed to our work, but this experience demonstrates how the transformation of a blighted property into a valued new asset may trigger optimism and new energy.

How did these housing-revitalization efforts fare? Twenty houses were rehabilitated and sold to Penn-affiliated households. We stabilized some premier blocks that were at risk. The decision to do a first-rate job, meticulously restoring the houses to their original charm, significantly increased their value and raised the bar on rehabilitation, especially for potential developers. In the end, this phase of the housing initiatives gave us further credibility in the neighborhood, a benefit that far outweighed the cost. By the year 2000, the market had grown strong enough to attract individual homeowners and developers who acquired, rehabilitated, and sold vacant houses on their own, without special program intervention requiring Penn resources.

The housing market was turning around. Potential homebuyers were coming from all over, spurred by the active University City market. Now the buyer who was looking at other affordable areas of the city—Queen Village and Bella Vista, for example—would investigate University City as well. Here were relatively inexpensive homes with backyards, ample parking on tree-lined streets, and, more important, the promise of rising property values. Many prospective buyers were ready to sign on the dotted line, right on the spot.

We were simultaneously revamping our guaranteed mortgage program with additional incentives to attract more Penn-affiliated homebuyers or encourage Penn-affiliated owners to improve their homes in the neighborhood. In 1998, the University introduced two new housing-incentive programs to demonstrate our commitment to West Philadelphia and our confidence in its future. In the first phase of the program, from 1998 to 2004, in addition to traditional mortgage guarantees provided by commitments from several lenders who entered into long-term agreements with the University, the Enhanced Mortgage Program for homebuyers provided a forgivable cash loan of $15,000, made available at mortgage settlement, or $21,000, available over a seven-year period, which could be used to pay closing costs or to fund home improvements (Figure 5). The loan was forgiven after the purchaser

Figure 5
Enhanced University City Mortgage Program and Rental Fund Sites.
John Kromer and Lucy Kerman, *West Philadelphia Initiatives: A Case Study in Urban Revitalization* (Philadelphia: University of Pennsylvania, 2004), p. 31.

had lived in the home for seven years. This was a crucial caveat—the house had to be the owner's primary residence. It was not a program for developers or investors. It was designed specifically to produce owner occupancy in the community. Imagine the lure of an affordable, grand, thirty-five-hundred-square-foot, three- or four-story Victorian home. Lead glass, decorative moldings and woodwork, and hardwood floors had great appeal, but these elegant features went hand in hand with years of neglect. The loans enabled prospective homeowners to renovate and modernize the houses.

The program expanded its home-buying boundaries in West Philadelphia, recognizing that homebuyers wanted and needed a variety of housing options, from large, attractive three-story homes to smaller, more efficient, and affordable homes. After March 31, 1999, the mortgage program no longer applied to houses in Center City, to reinforce the effort to enhance home ownership in West Philadelphia. Under the existing Guaranteed Mortgage Program, Penn faculty and staff buying homes in West Philadelphia could finance University-guaranteed mortgages at 120 percent, with up to 5 percent of that going for closing costs, and up to 15 percent applied to home repair or remodeling. Combining the Enhanced Mortgage Program and the Guaranteed Mortgage Program, a Penn-affiliated homebuyer who purchased in West Philadelphia had access to a mortgage guarantee and forgivable loan financing for closing costs and residential improvements, as well as a cash incentive. It was a great deal.

A new Home Improvement Loan Program made it easier for existing University-affiliated homeowners to improve their homes by upgrading or restoring porches, steps, doors, windows, and the decorative cornices that made these homes unique. From 1998 to 2004, this program enabled homeowners to borrow up to $7,500 interest free (to be matched by the owner), which could be used to fund eligible improvement costs. The owner's matching funds could be used for either exterior or interior improvements, but the University's portion could only be used for exterior improvements. The loan principal was forgiven at 20 percent annually over a five-year period, provided that the borrower continued to maintain the home as a primary residence.

Al Filreis, an English professor, was one of the first employees to take advantage of the new incentives, offering the asking price on a twin home, fully aware that there was a bidding war going on. University City had not seen a market like that in years. Filreis applied the full $15,000 incentive to finish the basement and took a 120 percent mortgage for other major work. Like many others, Filreis used local contractors and subcontractors, creating a boom for tradespeople in the immediate area. The matching funds for exterior home improvements added to the swell as Penn employees who were already area homeowners applied for the grants to fix leaky roofs or repair sagging porches.

By late fall 1998, the mortgage-guarantee program, in all its forms, stood at about $22 million outstanding. Administration and management responsibilities for all these programs were now centralized in Penn's Office of Community Housing, a resource center that hired professional staff capable of managing an ambitious program combining outreach, supportive services, and information about and referral to responsible mortgage lenders that offered fair rates to Penn-affiliated employees. Diane-Louise Wormley, who had helped develop our existing housing and mortgage programs, was named managing director for community housing, responsible for implementing the initiatives. The task for Wormley, a longtime resident and cheerleader for West Philadelphia, was to implement outreach geared toward marketing the neighborhood and supporting first-time homebuyers. The University developed strategies to identify and build relationships with resources and companies that could assist homeowners with home-improvement projects. For example, the Office of Community Housing assembled a database of tradespeople knowledgeable about Victorian homes and instituted home-buying seminars. It offered workshops on homeowner's insurance, family budgeting, asbestos awareness, and credit counseling and repair. In short, it did everything it could to help the homeowner, especially the first-time buyer. These services were available to all buyers, whether Penn affiliates or not.

In the first six months of the program, sixty-three houses were sold, and more than four hundred people participated in the mortgage workshops and/or counseling sessions between April and December. The Penn affiliates represented a cross section of the University, including faculty and staff, from a janitor in the housekeeping department to a vice president. A typical success story was Dorothy Darden, a forty-year-old woman employed in University housekeeping who had long dreamed of owning a home. Until she came in for homebuyer counseling, Darden figured that she would never qualify for a mortgage—homeownership was a pipe dream. Yet seven weeks after her first counseling session, she was the proud owner of a home to share with her extended family of adult children and their children, with mortgage payments lower than the monthly rent she had been paying. As word of success stories like this got out, the Office of Community Housing was bustling with inquiries.

Counseling was an integral part of the mortgage program, and every homeowner was required to complete housing counseling. Wormley has described the process as a combination of counseling on the front end and then constant handholding on the back end, something that had not been anticipated. Community Housing staff helped people with their credit rating, or with budgeting in order to make their mortgage payments. They tracked the portfolio listing of mortgages, and if a payment was late, someone would get on the phone and contact the homeowner to find out why and to offer assistance. Obviously, the University did not want to risk any defaults, especially with its own contingent liability. The handholding was effective: defaults were practically nonexistent.

University City realtors were thrilled with Penn's commitment. The housing market was heating up, with the best of the housing stock turning over rapidly. But the tough road was still ahead. The challenge was to retain the special character of University City with its unique blend of ethnic groups, varied incomes, and mix of housing options. We were striving to keep the neighborhood from gentrifying (or "Penntrifying," as our detractors liked to say).

The average home sale price in University City increased from $78,500 in 1995 to $175,000 in 2003, well above increases in house prices in Philadelphia and nationally. The volume of home sales more than doubled, from seventy-three in 1995 to 194 in 2003, with a significant number of homes placed under agreement of sale within ten days of listing. Some 386 Penn-affiliated households bought homes in University City between 1998 and early 2004, taking advantage of all the University-sponsored home-buying incentives. While 75 percent of these purchases involved mortgages of less than $150,000 and 40 percent were less than $100,000, there was great concern about gentrification. To combat this trend, we focused first on the affordable rental market and then on homeownership for smaller, single-family homes farther out into the neighborhood.

There was considerable agreement that the most direct way to address the threat of displacing lower-income residents was to maintain a supply of reasonably priced rental housing, especially housing focused on the nonstudent population. Long-term renters made up a significant portion of the lowest-income residents in University City, and we were determined to work to their benefit. Yet, the deterioration of the rental housing stock was a serious problem. Many apartment buildings were highly visible community eyesores. Vandalism and the threat of fire were real dangers. We had to determine how best to stop the deterioration of some of the worst "problem" properties. It was the only way to strengthen the rental market and stimulate additional reinvestment.

We understood that in the short term it was unreasonable to expect profitable results, no matter how cost consciously and efficiently managed the buildings were. The existing market was weak, and the buildings targeted for development had deteriorated badly. Still, we expected that a commitment of Penn funding in the early years would strengthen the market enough to attract private investment in subsequent years without further University intervention. Once again, we were looking at sustainable activities.

For Penn's situation at the time, pursuing development-subsidy financing through state or city government programs was not regarded as a viable strategy, for two reasons. As Kromer and Kerman indicate,

> the Commonwealth of Pennsylvania's primary rental housing program is the state-administered federal Low Income Housing Tax Credit (LIHTC) and a state-funded rental housing subsidy program known as PennHOMES. Both the tax credit program and PennHOMES are administered through the Pennsylvania Housing Finance Agency (PHFA). Neither of these programs was designed to support the development of a mix of neighborhood resident and student housing, and the underwriting and application processing associated with both programs would have reduced Penn's flexibility in implementing its program. Additionally, during the 1990s, the City of Philadelphia relied almost exclusively on U.S. Department of Housing and Urban Development (HUD) funding to support its housing programs, and most of the City-administered funding allocated to rental housing was used to leverage PHFA financing through the LIHTC and PennHOMES program.[5]

Also, the processes for budget allocation, proposal review, and project underwriting were extremely onerous. We did not feel that we could spare that much time.

Instead, we created a Neighborhood Housing and Development Fund in 1999. The fund was established to finance the rehabilitation and upgrading of a multimillion-dollar portfolio of rental properties acquired by Penn and its partners. We used a $5 million investment by Penn to attract other investors with "socially patient" capital. First in was Fannie Mae, the government-chartered mortgage/finance company, with $5 million, which was followed by funding commitments from nearby University of the Sciences in Philadelphia, Commerce Bank, and Trammell Crow, a real-estate-services firm (Citizens Bank has now replaced Trammell Crow and Fannie Mae). Penn and Fannie Mae were the general partners, and the other participants in the fund held limited partner positions.

The fund's goal was to acquire and renovate a targeted portfolio of up to twelve hundred rental units within an area bounded by Market Street, Woodland Avenue, 40th Street, and 49th Street. The fund acquired either highly visible buildings in deplorable condition or poorly managed properties that threatened the stability of the neighborhood. Site selection and development decisions were based on a number of factors that included choosing properties on blocks with little or no other housing vacancy and purchasing privately owned properties available through negotiated purchase. Initially the fund chose not to focus on tax sale or eminent domain acquisition, although over time it has relied on these as well.

The acquisition cost of the first five properties, with a total of 211 units, ranged from $21,200 to $52,000 per unit, with total capital improvement costs in the years between 2000 and 2002 ranging from $32,200 to $64,800 per unit. All of these buildings were inhabited by a mix of students (not all from Penn), working people, and people who were on welfare. The fund was intended to provide resources for both the purchase of affordable housing units and access to capital for repairs—fire escapes, fire-suppression systems, security for doors that had been broken for years. Fund investors expected their investments to stabilize and enhance blocks within the targeted area, prevent gentrification, and potentially generate some modest return on investment in the long run.

As soon as a building was purchased, a building-improvement plan was developed. The existing tenant base and condition in the real-estate market were evaluated, and appropriate rent adjustments were made. An asset manager for the fund was appointed to take responsibility for overseeing this effort. And to sustain a balanced tenant base, a percentage of the fund's overall portfolio was targeted for below-market rents.

The Cornerstone, a complex of three apartment buildings, is representative of the portfolio. Located in the Garden Court neighborhood, eight blocks from the western edge of the Penn campus, the Cornerstone is in a neighborhood that includes a mix of single-family homes, mid-rise apartments, and a small retail corridor. The buildings that made up the Cornerstone complex had hardwood floors, plaster walls, and crown molding, but they had suffered for years from poor management, with a backlog of deferred maintenance and code violations. After more than a year of negotiation, the fund purchased the properties for approximately $4.5 million, a per-unit acquisition cost of about $38,000. Life-safety issues were addressed first, which entailed removing an underground oil-storage tank, adding more lighting, and installing fire alarms and smoke detectors. Next, the buildings were upgraded by adding improved land-scaping and exterior lighting, repairing boilers, changing the plumbing, and updating the hallways and common areas. The hardwood floors were sanded and refinished, and the kitchens and bathrooms were re-furbished. The basic floor plans and configuration of the units remained unchanged. The total cost of the renovation was approximately $600,000. Today, rental rates are moderate, and although current student occupancy is slightly higher than previously, most tenants are neighborhood residents with no Penn affiliation.

Improvements in rental housing were not limited to fund-owned apartment buildings. Private investment increased in many sections of University City as the West Philadelphia Initiatives began to produce visible improvements in the neighborhood environment. A significant number of these privately financed ventures were small-scale building improvements with federal and city tax incentives that, taken as a whole, significantly upgraded the area's affordable rental-housing stock.

By the early years of the twenty-first century, the rental market had improved sufficiently to attract private investment in major rental-development ventures as well. Perhaps the crown jewel is the Left Bank, a 282-unit conversion to loft apartments of a formerly vacant industrial building east of the Penn campus, using tax credits designated for res-toration of historically significant properties. Completed in 2001, the Left Bank brought residents to an area of West Philadelphia that had been without residential living for decades (Figure 6).

Figure 6
The Left Bank sites, early 1990s
and 2002. (Top) Photo courtesy
of University of Pennsylvania
Department of Facilities Planning.
(Below) Photo by John Hubbard.

The Left Bank is an excellent model of creative reuse of historic, fallow properties that can transform a neighborhood and provide the identity that people are searching for when they move into an urban area. Lofts provide that connection not only through the revitalization of old buildings but also by restoring a way of life. Preservation and economics go hand in hand in loft projects like this, especially in cities and communities that offer economic incentives for restoration and rehabilitation. In the case of the Left Bank, the building had been an eyesore for many years and at various times was the scene of serious drug trafficking and music-club venues that led to many arrests and real concern for safety on the east end of our campus. Early in my term as president, we decided that we needed to buy the building as a tactical defense measure, and we hired an engineer to determine its condition. The engineering report advised us to take down the building. It was a huge warehouse with a steel-plate floor that was built to allow trucks to drive inside the building. Estimates for demolition came to $6 million. We could not justify that kind of money for demolition, so we ended up spending about $100,000 a year just to mothball it. But it was buildings just like this that developers were fighting over to convert into wonderful loft space and mixed-use units throughout New York City's Tribeca area. Returning one day from a trip to New York, I remarked to John Fry, "This is crazy. If they can do all of this redevelopment in New York and renovate the same kind of buildings as ours, why can't it happen here?"

By 2000, the real-estate market had begun to improve, and investors had more confidence in West Philadelphia as they saw the impact of the initiatives beginning to take hold. We put out a request for proposals to save the building and selected Carl Dranoff, at the time a relatively small (by usual standards) Philadelphia developer. But we admired the loft projects he had done and decided to take a chance on a local entrepreneur. We used a fixed, long-term ground lease approach that guaranteed Penn a payment sufficient to pay back the book value of the property. But the University still had to mitigate the environmental risks of the project, at a cost of $3 million, because the economics of the project could not absorb these costs. Our land value and this $3 million leveraged $55 million of development costs borne by Dranoff and his financial backers. It was a good choice. The Left Bank has won awards for historic restoration. And today, Dranoff's trend-setting properties are defining forces in the revitalization of many other neighborhoods in Philadelphia.

As the market improved further, the next several projects, described in the Appendix, attracted regional and national developers. No longer spending new dollars, Penn contributed the land value as equity to each project, with forty- to sixty-year reversionary ground leases, and it participates in the upside potential of each project.

As a second strategy to stem gentrification, in 2004 we modified Penn's housing incentives programs. In order to attract more low-income buyers, we extended the geographic coverage area of the mortgage and home-rehab programs to outlying West Philadelphia neighborhoods where the housing stock is more modest and affordable. And we closed off availability of the funds for the closer-in area that had become overheated. At the same time, we cut subsidies for the outer ring in half, reducing the maximum size of the forgivable cash loan from $15,000 to $7,500, because the housing stock in that area was far less expensive.

We launched a public-safety plan to include the outlying ring areas, enabling the University to attack crime trends in the newly targeted purchase areas. We had hoped-for success in extending the boundaries farther west to 52nd Street because there was a strengthened community to the north, thanks to a successful Community Development Corporation (CDC), which emanates from the People's Emergency Center (a social-services agency for homeless families headed by the very energetic and dynamic Gloria Guard).

A final component of the residential strategy is the construction of new units of graduate and undergraduate housing *on campus*. Apartment-like housing and the construction of a new College House on Hill Field (34th and Chestnut streets) will further decrease the demand for undergraduate student rentals off campus in West Philadelphia, thus freeing more housing stock to conversion for single-family, owner-occupied dwellings. While the construction takes place, creative swaps and condominium conversions are priming the pump.

For example, in a test case for swapping real estate at a time when we were unable to spend further resources on acquisition, we identified a set of properties that, if converted back to single-family units, would be ideal candidates for conversion because of their condition and their location in the Penn Alexander School catchment area (see Chapter 8). The owner of the four buildings specialized in student rental apartments and was not particularly interested in the single-family market. Penn approached him with the idea of swapping five multifamily buildings from our portfolio for his four strategically located buildings. A third-party appraisal firm provided the fair-market value of both sets of buildings. A deal was structured that was satisfactory to both parties, with the landlord paying an additional $25,000 per property to the University, since we were disposing of five properties in exchange for his four. And to motivate the landlord even further, we established an agreement in which both sets of multifamily properties would be managed by the landlord's property-management company for the duration of the leases held by the student renters. This provided an assurance that the properties would be kept in good shape during the several months of this process. If the landlord improved the efficiency of the properties over that time, Penn agreed to take the net improved value against the $25,000 surcharge on each property. But that would be capped at 50 percent, so no individual building could dip below a $12,500 surcharge on exchange. All in all, it was a deal that worked well for both parties. It is important to note that a deed restriction was put in place that would ensure that the properties acquired by Penn, once converted back to single-family use and sold, would remain zoned as single-family.

Maureen Kennedy and Paul Leonard theorize that if residents, developers, officials, and interest groups spent more time developing strategies to avert or address the adverse consequences of gentrification, and less time opposing or supporting the market-driven process itself, they could increase the chances of building strong, economically diverse communities in our cities.[6] This is something Penn tried hard to accomplish in University City. We planned for, and used structured approaches to achieve, a mix of housing options and a broad continuum of housing prices, including both owner-occupied units and rental properties in our initiatives. Nonetheless, the housing interventions did substantially increase area property values, which benefited long-time residents but at the same time placed a greater burden on hopeful prospective residents. On the plus side, we did not cause any involuntary displacement of original residents, which is a key feature of gentrification, according to Kennedy and Leonard. (The results of these initiatives are described more fully in the accompanying box.)

But if University City was to thrive, we also needed to rebuild its economic infrastructure, creating jobs and the retail amenities that were sorely lacking. In 1995, Harvard Business School professor Michael Porter wrote a fascinating essay with what many perceived as an unduly optimistic title, "The Competitive Advantage of the Inner City." Porter's argument was as bold as the title. He posited that "decades of social programs and interventions failed to halt the alarming decline of America's distressed urban neighborhoods . . . because they treated cities as charity cases that were best served by delivering social services and redistributing wealth."[7] What we really should be doing, he argued, is focusing on generating wealth in the inner city by establishing a sustainable economic base of viable, competitive businesses that create jobs, encourage entrepreneurship and investment, and serve the needs of what have been underserved neighborhoods.

At Penn, we had come to change our perspective about West Philadelphia in much the same way. We had stopped viewing University City as a liability that we had to minimize or a charity case that needed our aid. Instead, we saw a real economic opportunity, with partners willing to put effort and resources into a commercial transformation that could benefit everyone. Penn was spending millions a year on goods and services, and very little of this was filtering back into the community. It was time to change that. We would spur economic de-

Housing Initiative Results

HOME OWNERSHIP

Between 1998 and 2004, the Enhanced Mortgage Program supported a range of home purchases involving a diverse group of University-affiliated homebuyers.

✦ Of the 386 homes purchases supported through the program between 1998 and 2004, 291, or 75 percent, involved mortgages of less than $150,000 (40 percent under $100,000), with an average mortgage amount of $120,489.

✦ A total of 146 households participated in the Home Improvement Program between 1998 and 2004.

✦ The Enhanced Mortgage Program leveraged $48.57 million in private-lender mortgages through the end of 2003. The Home Improvement Loan Program leveraged almost $1.1 million in matching debt and equity financing for home repairs and modernization during the same period.

✦ Properties in University City appreciated 154 percent in value from 1994 to 2004. University City house prices grew at a substantially higher rate than prices for Philadelphia and the rest of the country during this period.

Although Penn's homeownership incentives were not the only factors influencing single-family sales and home improvements in University City, these incentives contributed significantly to the strengthening of the neighborhood real-estate market.

✦ Average sales prices of single-family houses rose from $78,500 in 1995 to $175,000 in 2003.

✦ According to local real-estate brokers, single-family homes for sale in the mid-1990s often remained listed and unsold for months. By 2003, the average number of days a home stayed on the market had dropped by 70 percent, with some houses under agreement of sale within days of initial listing.

RENTAL HOUSING

Through the capitalization of the fund to finance rental-property acquisition and upgrading, Penn has improved more than two hundred units of rental housing in University City since 2000. Buildings that had been significant community problems a few years before are now attractive, fully occupied, well-managed neighborhood assets. The renovated buildings returned to the rental market as a result of the University's intervention are occupied by a combination of tenants from the neighborhood and tenants from Penn.

Between 1998 and 2001, the proportion of graduate students renting in West Philadelphia rose from 23.8 percent to 28.6 percent. During this period, the proportion of Penn undergraduates living in West Philadelphia decreased, from 77.4 percent to 65.6 percent. These data suggest that, as planned, the student population of West Philadelphia neighborhoods grew slightly smaller and slightly older during these years as the rental-property inventory improved.

Improvements in rental housing were not limited to Penn-owned apartment buildings. As the implementation of the West Philadelphia Initiatives began to produce visible improvements in the neighborhood environment, private investment increased in many sections of University City. A significant number of these privately financed ventures were small-scale building improvements that, taken as a whole, significantly upgraded the area's rental housing stock. By the early years of the twenty-first century, the rental market had improved sufficiently to attract private investment in major rental-development ventures.

The Left Bank, a 282-unit conversion of a formerly vacant industrial building east of Penn campus to luxury apartments, was completed in 2002 as a privately developed, privately financed venture involving real estate that had been acquired and landbanked by Penn. University Crossings, the conversion of a long-vacant former office building northeast of the campus through a joint venture involving Drexel University and the Philadelphia Management Corporation, opened in the same year. The completion of these ventures illustrates the growing attraction of University City as a location for private investment and development following the implementation of the West Philadelphia Initiatives.

Current additional projects include Domus apartments (slated for occupation in fall 2007), a private-developer conversion of a 2.6-acre parking lot at 34th and Chestnut streets to 290 apartments and street-level retail stores. The University retained a sixty-five-year ground lease. Two portfolios of upper 40th Street properties are being developed (2006–2007) by private developers (Teres Holdings and the Metropolis Group) to create a mixed-use project yielding 120 residential units and 5,800 square feet of retail space.

Adapted from: John Kromer and Lucy Kerman, *West Philadelphia Initiatives: A Case Study in Urban Revitalization* (Philadelphia: University of Pennsylvania, 2004), pp. 28–29, 32–33.

velopment by building new retail establishments, by directing university contracts and purchases to local businesses, and by hiring locally, with special opportunities for women and minorities. And we would try to do so in such a way that everyone could be a winner.

CHAPTER 7

Invigorating the Local Economy

W HEN MY CLASS of '66 graduated from Penn, visiting families stayed in Center City hotels and partied at popular downtown restaurants like Bookbinder's. Nothing much happened near the campus, where the hippest places were Smokey Joe's, a popular watering hole, or the Dirty Drug, a neighborhood coffee shop of sorts, and you certainly did not take your parents to either of those.

Today, graduation at Penn means big business for University City. Families make reservations at one of several hotels (including our own Inn at Penn) or intimate bed-and-breakfasts in the vicinity. Not only can visitors find lodging right in the neighborhood, they can dine at a selection of some of the most diverse restaurants in greater Philadelphia, ranging from eclectic American, Italian, French, and Middle Eastern to Japanese, Senegalese, Ethiopian, and Mexican. A score of trendy shops with an array of stylish goods offer diversion from the festivities. To recent graduates, University City is a "happening" place, but just a decade ago it was basically a stretch of surface parking lots, empty since the popular but dingy restaurants of my era had been razed. Even more remarkable is the fact that underscoring this busy, vibrant destination is a healthy and vital local economy that once gasped for breath.

Whenever there is a story about the state of the economy or about economic forecasts—whether it is a sound bite on all-news radio or a comprehensive analysis in the *Wall Street Journal*—the leading indicator of economic trends is invariably consumer activity. Put simply, if we want to take the pulse of the economy, we examine the shopping receipts. Penn experienced the power of retailing firsthand. The institutional focus on retailing helped to drive efforts to revitalize West Philadelphia economically.

And because this was Philadelphia, underscoring that focus was a sense of pride in the city's place in retailing history and an awareness of the value of retailing. Philadelphia's own John Wanamaker founded the first department store in the United States by combining many specialty stores under one roof, an innovation that permanently changed retailing and the American shopping experience. It was also Wanamaker who gave us the memorable quote, "Half my advertising is wasted; I just don't know *which* half." Advertising aside, the presence of exciting retail establishments has drawn throngs of visitors to University City. It has kept the sidewalks busy and the housing market hot. By realizing the neighborhood's economic needs and creating businesses to fill those needs, Penn's investment in West Philadelphia has more than paid off.

We believed we could jump-start the economy because Penn had extraordinary buying power that was going elsewhere for lack of opportunities. Bringing business back to West Philadelphia was a critical element of building economic sustainability. In this, we subscribed to the thinking of Rolf Goetze, who wrote: "The most effective way of making neighborhoods self-supporting was to ensure that the interactions among provider, consumer, lender, investor, buyer, and seller and subsequent decisions by individual and institutional actors produce positive collective outcomes for neighborhoods."[1] And because we wholeheartedly believed in the importance of life on the sidewalks, we envisioned turning University City into a dynamic mix of residential and commercial life, suffused with the energy of urban university areas like Georgetown and Cambridge.

There is no doubt that new retail development can reenergize urban communities. It enlivens activity on the street, supports new business and job opportunities, and creates an interesting mixed-use neighborhood. But different neighborhoods require different kinds of support and, as an institution committed to neighborhood revitalization, Penn had to evaluate the balance of opportunity and risk from two perspectives: the type of retail that would generate the most buying power and the type of retail that would best reinforce the campus-neighborhood linkage. While it is true that a substantial portion of the retail expenditures of students might be captured by stores, restaurants, and other retail locations near campus, most faculty and staff did not live in the vicinity and might have preferred to shop in their own towns and neighborhoods. The academic calendar is another impediment. With so many prospective customers absent from campus during the summer months and for a portion of the winter holiday season—an especially critical time for merchants—one level of regular support for nearby retail sites is reduced. Thus, the retailers had to fulfill the needs of the neighborhood, as well as draw customers from nearby residential communities and elsewhere in the city, by offering a product mix that appeals to this broad customer base. And rather than erode the competitive position of existing community-based businesses, new retail ventures had to complement these products and services to round out the retail mix in the area.

It took careful planning, involving both campus and community constituencies. The goals were to create an appealing, strategically integrated, and complementary retail environment in the vicinity of the campus and out in the neighborhoods, to strengthen University City's competitive position as a retail destination for West Philadelphia residents and others. And through these activities, we hoped to reinforce the economic ties between the campus and its neighboring communities.

Three principles guided our planning. First, we would begin with a substantial commitment of University funding and staff resources to support initial development activity, with investments in major retail anchors that would be catalysts to attract private investment. Then, in subsequent ventures, Penn would reduce the level of its participation as the climate for private investment improved. Second, we would design the retail mix to invigorate its physical location. And third, drawing from the ideas of Frederick Law Olmsted, we would integrate open public space with retail establishments in order to enliven the streets.

Our approach to retail development involved extensive research and analysis to determine its feasibility, even as we dared to dream big dreams. The University's plan to lead the market by leveraging its resources to attract private development was a demonstration of what housing advocates Roger Ahlbrandt and Paul Brophy referred to as the "investment optimism" required for a successful neighborhood-revitalization strategy.[2] In 1997, we commissioned a supply-and-demand analysis, which used demographic data, on-site surveys, and information available through the International Council of Shopping Centers and other industry sources. It evaluated the potential for new retail development and concluded that by 2004 the primary trade area would be supported by a projected population of 47,800 people with an average household income of $38,000. After inventorying all the existing retail space, we applied industry formulas to determine that the primary trade area had the potential to support nearly four hundred thousand additional square feet of retail space. A full array of goods and services was deemed necessary, including apparel, furnishings, groceries, dining, and entertainment. It was further projected that residents and visitors would likely make about 65 percent of the purchases, and day workers and students who lived outside the trade area would make the remaining third. Additional studies evaluated existing traffic and retail patterns in the area.

To determine the specific types of retail establishments most desired within these categories, focus-group research was conducted with students and residents. We learned that students are more price sensitive with respect to consumer goods and clothing. They find stores that offer basics, such as socks and T-shirts, through major national retailers (e.g., Gap stores) most attractive, and they are less price sensitive about entertainment and eating and drinking expenditures. Students will readily spend money on these activities. Residents wanted the neighborhood to provide low-cost goods and services, and they especially wanted an area supermarket. Most of their shopping took place outside University City, but a significant number of respondents said they would shop locally if a wider variety of higher-quality retail establishments and national chain stores was offered.

Based on this extensive analytic work, we determined two main areas for reinforcing commercial development: on campus from 36th to 38th streets along the north side of Walnut Street (the south side was lined with academic buildings), and over to Sansom Street and the 40th Street corridor in the neighborhood. We focused on three major projects within these areas: Sansom Common, a complete retail complex from 36th to 37th and Walnut to Sansom streets, and two anchors—a movie theater and an upscale supermarket—on the north and south corners of 40th and Walnut Streets. Market research associated with planning for these anchors included projected annual sales of $15.5 million for a new supermarket. And despite the increasing popularity of videos and DVDs, movie-theater attendance across the country remained strong; the total U.S. box office grew at an average annual rate of 5.8 percent between 1993 and 1997. With only one movie theater in the neighborhood, there was certainly a market for another, especially the kind of theater we had in mind.

The usual financial parameters for returns on the University's investment in its endowment were not plausible in this case; we needed to establish much broader ones, and once again the vision and commitment of our trustees was laudable—and crucial. Besides using patient, social-investment rates of return, they allowed us to include a number of nonfinancial returns as metrics for success: an increase in median income in the area, an increase in Penn-affiliated residents in the area, a doubling of the volume of commercial and business activity in the area, and a marked increase in the value of noninstitutional real-estate holdings of the University. We would also need to leverage our own money with an expanded investment of private debt and equity that would build to the point of securing long-term viability of the neighborhood. In that respect, we were especially fortunate to receive the early support and backing of Fannie Mae, which validated our approach and enhanced our credibility as we forged critical partnerships with banks, foundations, local nonprofits, and neighboring institutions.

The two locations selected for development were intended to be distinctly different in their retail mix. Studies showed that the area inside the campus could support more upscale chain stores and restaurants. And although market research suggested demand for the addition of a supermarket and movie theater on the corners of 40th Street, it was a considerable challenge attracting new vendors to the 40th Street corridor, west of campus. The Community Builders, Inc., our development consultants, had evaluated the 40th Street corridor to determine the potential to expand the existing eighty-five-thousand-square-foot commercial business district. These blocks on 40th Street were heavily traveled but, as noted earlier, distinctly run-down. Even after our 40th Street Action Team had worked on improving the streetscape, many of the stores looked dated and had weak sales, although there were some viable businesses, including a bicycle shop, a Radio Shack, a number of carry-out restaurants, and a relocated Smokey Joe's, the same campus tavern that has catered to students since my own undergraduate days.

During the late 1990s, University and community representatives began discussing alternatives for preserving and improving this area. They concluded that the best revitalization approach for 40th Street would be one that reinforced and strengthened the area's international character and created a role as a meeting and gathering place. And it was decided to build capacity into the area in a way that would make it a significant catalyst for residential occupancy and further retail expansion in the adjacent neighborhoods.

Some of Penn's early moves were highly publicized, as when the 40th Street Action Team came in and spruced up 40th Street, announcing our intentions to be a leader in revitalizing this commercial corridor. One move that was less publicized, but no less valuable, was the hiring of a professional team to oversee and coordinate Penn's retail and economic development in West Philadelphia. The team included Jack Shannon, the former deputy director of commerce for the city of Philadelphia, and Tom Lussenhop, Penn's managing director of facilities and real-estate services. At one early meeting, executive vice president John Fry asked Shannon to lead the effort to deal with the nearly one hundred curbside food vendors (many in large, smoke- and noise-spewing trucks) who lined the streets of campus. Vendors at Penn were a long-standing tradition, offering quick service and cheap food to the University community. To their supporters, the vendors provided a valuable service, could do no wrong, and were within their rights to operate in a free economy. To their detractors, the vendors were a public nuisance and a health and safety risk. The truth was somewhere in between. In his first eighteen months on the job, Shannon worked with Carol Scheman, vice president of government and community public affairs, and focused considerable time on finding a workable compromise between the vendors and the University.

For the most part, the vendors were hard-working, licensed individuals trying to earn a living. But they were in violation of city laws that prohibited all-day parking. From the perspective of the police, the vendors created three potential dangers. Many of them used propane-gas and/or gasoline-powered electrical generators. Scheman watched from her window one day as huge flames shot out of a vending cart below. The risk of explosion, especially if one of the trucks was struck during an auto accident, was substantial. Second, the trucks blocked sight lines. Like students everywhere, Penn students tend to jaywalk. There were too many accidents or near accidents as students stepped out between the trucks only to be met by a car or bicycle. Third, many vendors lacked adequate sanitation facilities.

The vending trucks presented another significant problem from the perspective of retail development: their presence on the streets was detrimental to a quality retail atmosphere, and contributed especially to the lack of restaurants. Clearly, it was time for an ordinance to regulate the operation of the vending trucks on the streets targeted for new retail stores. It was not our intention to eliminate vendors from University City. We had respect for the vendors, and a photograph of a vending truck dating back to the early 1900s hung in John Fry's office. We wished to preserve the tradition, but we also wanted to regulate what constituted an unofficial industry, to make it safer, cleaner, and more attractive as well as accessible, while allowing a broader base of retail establishments to develop. It was a question of striking the right balance.

Working with the City Council, we began a concerted effort to do something about the vending trucks. We met with community groups to discuss solutions and organized meetings with the vendors, many of whom were angry and anxious about their future. We listened to groups within the University, vendor advocates (including both students and faculty), and vendor opponents (including the director of Penn's Van Pelt Library, who had a concern about the many vendors directly behind his building). Graduate students, who tend to eat on the run and relied on the vendors for inexpensive meals and a place to meet, were especially irate. Eventually, the opening of a Graduate Student Center in 2001, which provided a space to eat, congregate, and study right on Locust Walk (a main pedestrian artery) in the heart of campus, dispelled some of that resentment.

John Fry came up with the idea of fresh-air food plazas, and we ultimately invested in a number of these, which moved the vending trucks from unsafe locations on the city streets to designated areas on campus, and cleared the way for successful retail development. The plazas provided water, electricity, sanitary refuse removal, and a more attractive and safer environment for the vendors as well as their patrons.

Some 80 to 90 percent of the vendors remain in the fresh-air food plazas on campus today. Some left of their own volition. Some became successful entrepreneurs with Penn's help: the Crepe Man now has a large booth in Houston Hall (the student union), and the Greek Lady now has a restaurant on 40th Street. A successful outcome of the vendor issue also depended heavily on our relationship with the City Council and with elected and appointed officials in the community, relationships that we had been building through other significant outreach efforts.

With the vending trucks cleared from Walnut Street and 36th and 37th streets, we were able to begin construction on our first ambitious retail project. Sansom Common, a $95 million mixed-use development project completed in 1999, was the largest commercial investment in West Philadelphia history (Figure 7).

When the University first announced plans to be the sole investor in Sansom Common in order to transform an unsightly (and, at night,

Figure 7

Sansom Common site, early 1990s and 2002.

(Top) Photo by James R. Mann. (Below) Photo by John Hubbard.

menacing) surface parking lot into a retail area, the reaction was not all favorable. The Faculty Senate questioned the use of university resources in this instance much more than in the case of investments in the "clean and safe" plan and housing initiatives. Some accused us of wanting to turn Penn into a shopping center. As Omar Blaik recalls, "It was not a value everyone understood. So the cynics took the higher moral standing by saying, 'I'm not sure why we should take $19 million away from the College and build a shopping center when that is not what our core mission is.'"[3]

But this was not about promoting retail establishments per se, it was about changing quality of life and increasing the economic capacity of the neighborhood. New retail development was expected to energize empty streets with increased foot traffic and nightlife, enhancing public safety. It was expected to create new job opportunities and be a magnet for our neighbors. And if we could make this a destination for tourists and campus visitors, or bring in shoppers from other areas, well, better still. We probed these assumptions deeply with the leadership of the faculty and the deans. We also shared financial data with them regarding the costs of the retail program and the expected returns. Good, tough questions led to more refined analysis by our real-estate team, and we came to rely more and more on the deep expertise of the faculty and benefited from their probing. Excluded critics became critical partners, and every element of these initiatives was improved through both faculty skepticism and faculty support. But it was never easy.

In the initial planning stages for the retail development, the proposed bookstore also became a topic of great campus debate, which was not surprising, considering that over the past twenty years there had been numerous proposals for a new bookstore. An inadequate "temporary" bookstore had been standing for decades. In 1990, for example, the University had announced a plan to build the Revlon Center, a two-hundred-thousand-square-foot multipurpose center incorporating the bookstore's growing needs in a complex that would also house performing arts and other student activities. The Revlon Center, which would be located at 36th and Walnut streets, would extend the "center" of campus to the north, with 36th Street closed between Walnut and Sansom streets. When I arrived at Penn in 1994, plans were already under way for the Revlon Center (named for the cosmetics company of its donor, Penn alumnus Ronald O. Perelman), which was to be completed by 1996. As projected costs soared, many at Penn also came to see that it would be a terrible mistake to move the student center away from the very heart of campus, the hundred-year-old Houston Hall (the nation's oldest student union). Plans for the Revlon project were stopped. Instead, the plan for the new campus center was to restore its original site, creating Perelman Quad, which was designed by the firm of Venturi, Scott Brown. In effect, the Quad created a second Locust Walk (a main campus gathering place) by restoring and linking four architecturally significant buildings, tied together by a newly constructed, vibrant public space to keep the center of student activity in the historic part of the campus.

By developing Perelman Quad, we were able to salvage some of Penn's most beloved and historic buildings that were in danger of falling into functional oblivion. One of these was Irvine Auditorium, an architectural treasure that was restored to a grandeur that befits its eleven-thousand-pipe Curtis Organ, the eleventh-largest pipe organ in the world. The organ, which was built for the nation's Sesquicentennial Exhibition in 1926, was donated to the University in 1928. Houston Hall, the student center, was renovated to accommodate Houston Market, a popular campus eatery, and a raft of student activities. Fortunately, Perelman threw his support behind the concept of the Quad, doubling his original pledge for this new project.

But the placement of a new bookstore remained an issue, and by the time we started to work on our retail strategy, it had become the focus of considerable debate. Should we replace the existing bookstore at 38th and Walnut streets? Should it front Locust Walk, the University's primary east-west pedestrian corridor? Should it go in the vacant church on Walnut Street just west of 40th Street, giving it a grand character? In its plan for developing the 40th Street corridor, The Community Builders, our consultant, recommended putting the bookstore on 40th Street, in order to establish an anchor for the commercial corridor where the campus meets the community and to act as a catalyst for revitalization.

At one point early in the planning process, before Penn contracted with Barnes and Noble, an executive of a large British chain of bookstores interested in joining Penn on this project paid a visit. Our representative took him to lunch at a popular local French restaurant, where the two enjoyed a classically rich meal. Later, they took a stroll up Walnut Street, beginning at 34th Street and heading toward 40th Street, the potential site for the new bookstore, past an increasingly deteriorated commercial streetscape. The farther they walked from campus, the more deflated the businessman became. Finally, they reached 40th Street, dingy and rundown. At this point, the elegant gentleman leaned against the street post and lost his lunch. Perhaps he was reacting to the rich meal rather than the location, but the impeccable timing of his distress was cause for wonder.

Ultimately we concluded that the bookstore should, symbolically, be closer to the center of the campus. Creating Sansom Common provided a terrific opportunity to transform the area and reinforce the energy of campus, encouraging a flow of campus pedestrian traffic out into public streets. Anchoring the commercial complex was the Penn Bookstore (operated by Barnes and Noble, which paid about half of the construction costs), which opened in 1998 on the corner of 36th and Walnut streets. Combining the elements of a full-service academic bookstore with the amenities of a Barnes and Noble superstore, at thirty thousand square feet it was the largest Barnes and Noble campus bookstore in the country. Throughout the store, murals and kiosks depict favorite images and the rich history of Penn. To customers, the availability of an ATM machine and the sale of tokens and transit passes for public transportation are valued services. A delightful children's corner is a favorite of the community. Outside, the sidewalk was widened and tables and chairs were added, extending to a newly constructed neighboring café. Across the street at 36th and Sansom streets, where a small but unsightly parking lot used to sit, a minipark now welcomes people with more tables and chairs. In fair weather, a jazz band plays on Thursday evenings. In other elements of the project, shoppers now have access to such retailers as Ann Taylor Loft, the Gap, and Urban Outfitters. The University-owned retail establishments have animated the streets and helped to bolster the school's image. What's more, these businesses are hugely successful; by 2004, they were generating $65 million in revenue annually, which translates to additional tax revenue for the city—definitely a win-win situation.

In 1999, the University added to the Sansom Common complex the Inn at Penn, an upscale, 238-room hotel with eighteen thousand square feet of meeting space, managed by Hilton Hotels. The Inn covers most of the block bounded by 36th, 37th, Walnut, and Sansom streets above the retailers just described. When the hotel opened, the block was still called Sansom Common, but for some reason, the name never quite caught on. In fall 2002, we began a marketing campaign and changed the name to University Square. Bright banners with the University Square logo now mark the hub of the commercial corridor. Even though the University is not everyone's landlord, the University Square promotion includes all the businesses from the 3400 block of Sansom Street, where our efforts to raze the block in the 1970s had encountered such resistance. With Penn's more enlightened sense of community partnership, it is natural to promote these small, independent businesses. (In fact, valet services for these establishments now use University parking garages.)

While the Sansom Common project came off with few hitches and generated the buzz that we had hoped for, the $75 million 40th Street project would challenge even the most resolute among us. At the periphery of the campus at 40th and Walnut streets, we bought out the lease for a Burger King to make way for the construction that we hoped would breathe new life into 40th Street and create true convergences between town and gown: a state-of-the-art movie theater and a very desirable food market. While we took the lead in envisioning the project and investing our own capital, we insisted on getting both the food market and the cinema operators to invest as well. It was an exciting time. There was enormous energy flowing, and we felt as though we were on a roll.

Of the two proposed anchor projects, the one that got tremendous press coverage was the deal Penn inked with Robert Redford and Sundance Cinemas in 1998 to build a movie theater that would show independent and experimental films. The theater would feature an art gallery and café, a video library, community meeting spaces, and perhaps a jazz club. Redford and I met on numerous occasions, and we talked for hours about the look of 40th Street. I frequently joked that my stock with parents, especially the mothers of our students, went up considerably once the newspaper showed us together on the Friday of Family Weekend. I couldn't help being amused when several moms approached me, not to discuss academics or their children but to ask what Redford was really like.

Redford was the one who convinced us about the look of the theater on the southwest corner of 40th and Walnut streets. Preliminary designs by our consultants incorporated both the elements of the neighborhood's Victorian architecture and Penn's Georgian red brick, but Redford was more visionary in his approach. He imagined a stunning contemporary design, one that would draw attention and light to the commercial corridor, adding more dynamism to the neighborhood. He urged using the same designer for the new food market (with an eight-hundred-car parking garage above it) that would anchor the northwest corner. On the southeast corner stood the vacant Walnut West branch of the Philadelphia Free Library, a beautiful classical-style building and Philadelphia's first Carnegie library. Redford loved the idea of the library with its hundred-year history as the third anchor. However, in 1996, the library had been closed because of flooding, and it was in such disrepair that it was headed for demolition. The library was later rescued by the community, which rallied hard to keep it standing. Because of our strategic goals for 40th Street, Penn contributed significantly to the fundraising campaign for the library and provided free temporary space for the collection while the building underwent extensive renovation. Its new interior is stunning, a contemporary design that excites and energizes its visitors. When the library reopened in September 2004, the ceremony featured Penn students together with neighborhood children walking into the renovated building carrying the books back into their new home.

It was Redford who introduced us to Carlos Zapata, the Venezuela-born partner of Wood and Zapata Architects of Boston, the same group that later designed the new Soldier Field stadium, home to the Chicago Bears. Zapata's designs for the movie theater and the supermarket provided the sizzle we were looking for—warm woods and expansive glass, jutting angles and curves. They were bold, sleek, and innovative. The Penn campus had its own majesty, but 40th Street was to be a staging ground for commercial expansion and for cementing town-gown relations. A new look was needed to energize the streets and signal a new era.

Some of our trustees were steadfast in their perception of Penn as a red-brick campus and believed it should stay that way. However, as those in favor of the new look pointed out, there were buildings on campus that were clearly not red brick. The president's and provost's offices were in College Hall, in the heart of campus, which was a model of the green tones of the Victorian period. And many of us felt that the standard red brick used so liberally in the 1960s and 1970s to try to replicate the early American era was in fact a poor choice. Had another material been used in its place, those modern buildings, including the library, might not have appeared so sterile and unattractive. (We did later work on those exteriors to improve the facades.)

It was clear that Zapata was not going to work in red brick. Over the course of several meetings with the facilities committee, faculty and trustees came to agree that we had to have a mix of traditional and innovative, edgy architecture if Penn was going to be the innovative, entrepreneurial school that they wanted it to be. After all, this was the school of Louis Kahn and other architectural and planning luminaries. This spirited dialogue led to the creation of a design-guideline manual for all future construction at Penn.[4] Basically, the guidelines called for more traditional architecture close to the center of campus. The farther from the center of campus, the more experimental and differentiating the architecture could be, much like the award-winning chiller plant

Figure 8

Fresh Grocer site, early 1980s and 2003. (Top) Photo courtesy of University of Pennsylvania Department of Facilities Planning. (Below) Photo by John Hubbard.

on the east edge of campus. For example, the new McNeil Center for Early American History on Hill Field at the corner of 34th and Walnut streets, designed by Robert A. M. Stern (which opened in 2005), is a very traditional, elegant, and wonderful red-brick edifice. In a fresh twist on conventional appearance, the new Skirkanich Hall on 33rd Street designed by New York's Tod Williams and Billie Tsien & Associates, a fifty-eight-thousand-square-foot bioengineering building (opened in 2006), is constructed of a green brick material. Designed to blend with its setting among the trees, Skirkanich Hall is not quite what some of the trustees were thinking of when they insisted on brick buildings, but it is a marvel, nonetheless.

But no red brick for the 40th Street corridor! Having already won many awards for historic renovation for the Furness Building and all the buildings of Perelman Quad, we were ready to take on the modern vocabulary of Carlos Zapata, literally and figuratively on the edge (of campus). The new food market would offer an enormous array of prepared and organic foods as well as standard supermarket fare and staples. When the Fresh Grocer opened in 2000, it transformed a corner once dominated by a surface parking lot, fast-food restaurants, and discount stores (Figure 8). The store—all forty-five thousand square feet of it—is open twenty-four hours a day 365 days a year, making it a draw for students, hospital workers, and others with late-night hours. As a result, Fresh Grocer bustles with activity round the clock. At lunchtime, flocks of customers choose from a huge selection ranging from veggie wraps and sushi to home-style favorites like macaroni and cheese or fried chicken. In the evening, the mezzanine-level café is filled with students studying and neighbors socializing, and in nice weather the tables outside are filled. You can walk into the store any time, even at three in the morning, and there is always someone shopping. Some thirty thousand people stop at Fresh Grocer each week, and at the checkout counter you are as likely to see customers with food stamps as those with Prada wallets, a testimonial to the diversity of the neighborhood.

The food market and garage generated not only excitement but also our first taste of extensive design and construction changes ordered by the prospective tenant, with more than $3 million in cost overruns and delays. It was far less fun being a developer this time. Profits from the successful Sansom Common project evaporated, and lawsuits threatened to replace champagne-drenched openings. (Ultimately some of this money was recovered through successful legal action.) And while we were sorting out the mess and construction was proceeding on the movie theater, the unthinkable happened. The parent company, General Cinema, filed for bankruptcy in 2000 and pulled the plug on the Sundance Theater project, shattering our plans along with our egos. What to do with the unfinished, vacant building at the corner of 40th and Walnut streets? We did not have many options. We were not the only ones who suffered from the multiple bankruptcies that hit the cinema industry, which is why we were knocking on doors along with twenty other real-estate developers, all in the same position. Although the cinema market had stabilized somewhat after the turmoil of 2000 and 2001, companies that did survive were busy consolidating and restructuring. No local operator possessed either the capital or the appetite to invest or expand.

If we withdrew from the cinema project, many would interpret this as a withdrawal of our support from a critical crossroad between the University and its neighborhood, a message we were loath to send. Once again the trustees gave us the elbow room and resources to figure out the right solution. We weighed the net financial burden of mothballing the project against building and operating a cinema. Even if the most pessimistic parameters were considered, it was costly but less expensive to complete the cinema than to abandon the project. And the financial stakes were high for Penn's real-estate portfolio as well. Abandoning the project and leaving the building vacant would undoubtedly hurt the value of the University's commercial holdings in the neighborhood, particularly those in the immediate proximity of the theater. The arguments against additional investment were also strong, particularly since the cash on cash return (the property's annual net cash flow divided by the net investment) was now much lower than originally projected.

Understandably, some again admonished Penn for biting off more than it could chew. This time I worried they were right. But we were fortunate, and another partner eventually emerged. National Amusements, a division of Viacom, was joining with Paul Heth, an independent international operator, and Dana Lee, the well-known international architect behind many of the W-Hotels, to create a new concept for movie theaters called the Bridge, an upscale, service-oriented, sophisticated movie-going environment. The Bridge intended to appeal to more discriminating niche audiences who wanted to see both art and commercial films but had become alienated from the mass-market approach of most suburban theaters. At the first Bridge, in Los Angeles, theatergoers could see foreign films like *Amélie* and *The Full Monty*, commercial films like *Harry Potter* and *A Beautiful Mind*, and specialty films like *The Royal Tenenbaums* and *Gosford Park*. The state-of-the-art auditoriums and screening equipment, ergonomic seating, and concession and lounge offerings were consistent with high-quality theater experience. It was moviegoing at the height of comfort and convenience, with reserved ticketing, restroom attendants, and parking facilities—an environment that would be unique in Philadelphia.

With extraordinary hard work on the part of John Fry and Omar Blaik, National Amusements was ultimately willing to commit to a fifteen-year lease and $3.3 million capital investment in the project (Penn added another $2 million). National Amusements could have chosen almost any city, so it says a lot about the vision of its CEO (and Penn parent) Shari Redstone that the corporation was drawn to the idea of this project as a neighborhood-campus connector. She remained a great supporter and friend as this project took its inevitable share of bumps and growing pains. Clearly a university's friends are crucial assets when it attempts difficult undertakings.

Less than two years after the Sundance project collapsed, the Bridge Cinema de Lux, a state-of-the-art movie-theater complex, opened at 40th and Walnut streets to rave reviews, with a reception that included a glistening ice sculpture of a movie camera (Figure 9). The Bridge is the first theater of its kind on the East Coast and offers such amenities as a multimedia art gallery, where theatergoers and restaurant patrons can watch short subjects, movie trailers, and behind-the-scenes footage from popular films, as well as a separate area to show student animations and videos. There are also wireless Internet facilities and a library in the lounge area, available to anyone. In addition to these amenities, the Bridge runs programs to attract the West Philadelphia and Penn communities, such as Bookworm Wednesday, a summer program that exchanged movie tickets for book reports, allowing both parents and children to attend.

Figure 9

The Bridge site, early 1980s and 2003. (Right) Photo by James R. Mann. (Below) Photo by John Hubbard.

Free validated parking at the parking garage across the street helps to draw theatergoers from all over the city and the suburbs. Its name could not be more fitting, because the new theater represents both a connection and a place of convergence between town and gown. It is no wonder that the Bridge attracts more than half a million patrons a year.

In 2004, the theater was finally completed the way Zapata designed it, with the addition of the Marathon Grill, a popular Philadelphia eatery. Now huge horizontal slabs of lustrous wood complement the sleek glass facade, and the feel is a mixture of cosmopolitanism and comfort, as befits the budding commercial district.

With two successful anchors to 40th Street in place, we continued with our commitment to develop the 40th Street corridor and to boost small-business ownership (Figure 10). We wanted to capitalize on the enormous diversity that exists in locally grown businesses and projects. This vision, culled by many discussions with community representatives dedicated to preserving and improving the area, was to develop a commercial corridor that would provide entertainment, arts and culture, and services to both the campus and the community and do so in a way that was special, with the character, style, diversity, and energy that are created when merging university and community. Most important, we did not want to develop this corridor haphazardly. Andres Duany makes the point in "The New Urbanism and the Center Cities" that city leadership could take a lesson from suburban management, particularly with regard to retail development.[5] In a shopping center, every store is recruited proactively. He contends that the newest shopping center would fail within months if it were managed as randomly as the typical main street. It was a mistake we did not want to make.

We intentionally recruited a variety of ethnic restaurants, art galleries, a student-run performance center, a used-book store, a used-CD and used-record store, and a yoga studio. Now along the 40th Street corridor there is a gallery space run by a Penn graduate, a French bakery, a vintage-comic-book and vintage-record store, and Ben & Jerry's, in its first University City location. While some small retailers have complained about the bureaucracy that needs to be navigated to get

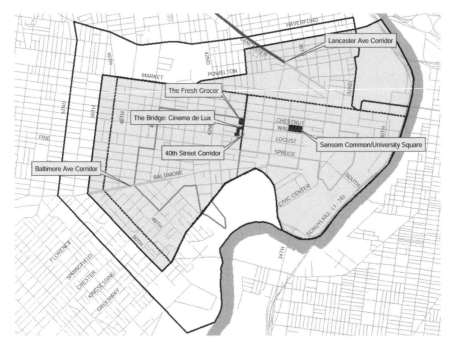

Figure 10

Locations of Retail Revitalization Activities. John Kromer and Lucy Kerman, *West Philadelphia Initiatives: A Case Study in Urban Revitalization* (Philadelphia: University of Pennsylvania, 2004), p. 35.

approval to open a store on the 40th Street corridor, Penn's commitment to creating sustainable retail establishments has, for the most part, been successful. The University provided technical support, for example, to the owners of Fatou & Fama, a restaurant featuring Senegalese cuisine. After Penn's help in drafting a business plan, the owners were able to obtain private financing for start-up expenses. The restaurant opened in 2002 on Chestnut Street, just west of 40th Street, and has become a popular and successful addition to the local restaurant scene. It is patronized by a mix of students, faculty, and local residents and exemplifies the diversity of the neighborhood.

In the early phase we gave free studio and residential space to artists willing to move into the area, recognizing, like the scholar Richard

Florida, who studies the elements that make for creative communities, that artists draw diverse, creative residents and businesses.[6] By 2004 we had brought the Philadelphia International Film Festival and the famous Fringe Festival to West Philadelphia. Synergies with academic programs increased as Penn's Film Studies Program expanded and leveraged resources and visibility from the activities. Arts students interacted with the influx of professional artists in the new studio spaces; the movie theater had a special free viewing room for video and animation clips created by Penn students. Student interest in the arts kept increasing, fueled in part by the dynamic arts community that was growing in the neighborhood.

In 2004, the University moved to a new phase for the continuing development of the 40th Street corridor. Penn Praxis, the student-faculty clinical consulting practice in Penn Design, was called upon to lead a new community-wide effort in creating shared planning principles for the future development of 40th Street farther to the north and to the south from Baltimore Avenue to Filbert Street. These plans included developing upstairs space for rental apartments to increase residential occupancy on this corridor (and to provide more "eyes on the street") and offering technical support to assist new businesses with property improvements and business financing, as we had done with Fatou & Fama. Much like the legal clinics most law schools operate for future lawyers, Penn Praxis gives students in the design school the opportunity to gain real-world problem-solving experience while helping community and civic groups that cannot afford professional services. At a series of public forums, representatives of University City's rich diversity—from local merchants and neighbors to the west and north, to Penn students, and even our fiercest critics—hashed out their ideas. Penn is, by intent, now only one voice among many.

The work on 40th Street complements that being undertaken by the University City District on Lancaster Avenue and Baltimore Avenue, two major commercial corridors that diagonally bisect University City's residential neighborhoods (Figure 10). To assist local businesses and business associations, UCD has hired full-time managers assigned to each of these two corridors. The corridor manager serves as a resource to support planning, marketing, and area promotion activities sponsored by the local business community, as well as to provide direct assistance to individual businesses and facilitate access to government programs and municipal services.

Penn's economic development plan had a second key pillar to complement the first of constructing and attracting retail amenities. It was to build sustainable economic capacity back into the neighborhood by providing new opportunities for local nonretail businesses, producing a multiplier effect that would encourage more business development and increase job growth among neighborhood residents. A linchpin of this strategy was the establishment of University goals for economic inclusion.

Historically, only a small portion of Penn's annual $650 million purchase of goods and services benefited local businesses. That had to change if we were going to fulfill the mission of stimulating a sustainable local economy. There was no doubt that we needed to develop and execute a comprehensive plan for minority and community contracting, purchasing, and employment. We understood that not only was this important as an economic stimulus, but that no institutional program to address the effects of economic disinvestments in the neighborhood would be regarded as credible without a clearly articulated, well-managed policy in support of minority and community contracting, purchasing, and hiring.

It was exciting to ask ourselves, "How can we deploy our purchasing more strategically?" We planned an economic-inclusion program designed to leverage the University's purchasing power and business relationships to facilitate enhanced business and job opportunities in West Philadelphia. The goal of the program was to contribute to a more economically prosperous community by increasing spending with community-based and minority-owned businesses. It had a number of components, including: stimulating major business relocation to and expansion within University City, building on Penn's purchasing relationships, and increasing the employment of community and minority residents on University-sponsored construction and other projects. We knew that in order to achieve these goals, the University's messages to the community regarding its commitment to economic inclusion had to be both consistent and demonstrable. The University needed to work closely with community constituencies concerned about economic inclusion. In addition, the concepts of the economic-inclusion program had to be embedded into Penn's culture.

Penn had been directing a portion of its purchases toward West Philadelphia vendors through a "Buy West Philadelphia" program developed to identify and purchase products from local vendors. Although the University had promoted this program as well as a "Hire West Philadelphia" campaigns for years, there had been no emphasis on measuring the impact of these efforts in quantifiable terms and no real ownership or accountability for these programs. A number of other factors kept the participation low. Minority and community-based suppliers of goods and services often lacked the resources to compete successfully for Penn's vending and service contracts, which required a complicated and lengthy bidding process. Local and minority subcontractors failed to bid on, or gain, construction work because they lacked access to unionized trades and had insufficient working capital and bond coverage.

To combat these obstacles to inclusion Penn developed a three-pronged approach. We created a University-wide policy with broad applicability, documented and monitored institutional performance in addressing economic-inclusion issues, and provided specialist assistance as needed to enable small vendors to compete effectively for University business.

An economic-opportunity plan was developed with the assistance of the Greater Philadelphia Urban Affairs Coalition (GPUAC), a local diversity consultant with a lot of experience in this work. We continued to employ them for assistance with the implementation and the monitoring of the plan. One of their excellent recommendations was to appoint an advisory committee on economic inclusion, which we formed in 1998. This advisory committee was cochaired by Penn's vice president for business services, Lee Nunnery, and its director of community relations, Glenn Bryan, both of whom lived in the neighborhood. Representatives from other university operating departments, including

Facilities and Real Estate Services, Purchasing, and Penn Medicine, sat on the committee, as their units had the greatest annual expenditure on construction, goods, and services. Importantly, the committee also included community leaders, local clergy, elected officials, and contractors. Its goal was to design activities that would increase the level of participation of minority workers and minority-owned businesses in Penn-related spending.

A formal Economic Opportunity Program was developed by 2000, to guide contracting and employment associated with Penn-sponsored construction projects. It applied to any construction project exceeding a cost of $5 million and specified goals for the participation of minority and community firms and residents. These goals became part of the contract documentation between Penn and the construction manager and general contractor for each project subject to the policy. The plan required that construction contractors make good-faith best efforts to support minority and community contracting and employment. To give it force, the guidelines provided for withholding of progress payments should a noncompliance issue arise. Contractor performance was monitored by the advisory committee on economic inclusion.

GPUAC set goals for awarding of contracts and employment of residents that were challenging but realistic, based on industry and marketplace conditions. They monitored a number of discrete, quantifiable variables, including payroll records for hiring and employment retention, the subcontractor bidding process, and purchasing records.

But setting and monitoring goals, while necessary, was not sufficient. It was critical to offer supportive actions and technical assistance to help minority and community subcontractors and suppliers to compete successfully. The University became actively engaged in a number of areas to facilitate this goal. Working with GPUAC and local community leaders and elected officials, Penn helped sponsor pre-apprentice and skills training programs for construction, retail, and hospitality employment opportunities for University City. In a collaborative effort with the West Philadelphia Partnership, the Community College of Philadelphia, community groups, and individuals, the University created a Skills Development Center at University City High School to provide area residents with comprehensive job training that would have direct and immediate applicability in the new kinds of commercial ventures being cultivated in the community.

We also helped community entrepreneurs create middleman companies to deal with large vendors, mentoring (often with the volunteer assistance of Wharton faculty and students) these small businesses to forge partnerships with major national firms, such as IKON Office Solutions, Fisher Scientific, and Staples. In April 1995, I was privileged to participate with local dignitaries and business people in a press conference to announce $2.8 million in new business contracts intended to benefit West Philadelphia's economy. The announcement of these partnerships was received with great enthusiasm.

The story of Todd Rose, an African American local businessman and West Philadelphia resident, illustrates the success of this enterprise. Rose heads Telrose, Inc., an office-equipment firm. Previously, he had been a sales representative for Xerox Corporation and, in the course of marketing Xerox products to Penn customers, had learned of Penn purchasing programs aimed at promoting new minority-owned and West Philadelphia–based businesses. Rose had taken advantage of this opportunity to go into business in the fall of 1994, establishing Rose Computer Systems, Inc. In the first year and a half, his sales to Penn hit the $1.5 million mark. That growth enabled his company to service other large clients and to do so by using mostly local talent. He later formed Telrose Corporation, and in late 2001 that company partnered with Datrose Corporation of Rochester, New York. The new company competed with major mail-services firms through a request-for-proposals process and was selected to serve as the residential mail provider for Penn's entire College House system. The partnership brought the University leading-edge technical solutions and a high quality of human resource management techniques, with an emphasis on hiring from the community. In fact, 99 percent of Telrose staff is from West Philadelphia. And Penn now has a vastly improved mail system and improved internal business processes.

Some of the changes in the way we did business came from simply observing practices at the University. When I arrived, for example, I noticed that the food at campus receptions and functions did not vary much from event to event. I learned that only a few caterers were approved for Penn business. There were many local caterers, just as there were local graphic artists and other small vendors who were not getting our business or our attention. In an effort to extend opportunities to local vendors and minority- and women-owned businesses, Penn Business Services Division, through its Supplier Diversity program, now provides a mechanism to handle these individual vendors and to get to know them. No longer do these vendors hand their business cards to someone, all the while knowing that the perfunctory "we'll be in touch" will never happen. Now a range of eclectic caterers service campus functions, and a much broader selection of West Philadelphia vendors do business with the University.

The economic impact of this inclusive approach to procurement, construction, and employment is significant, with measurable benefits to the neighborhood, city, and region. In fiscal year 1996, Penn purchased $20.1 million in goods and services from West Philadelphia suppliers and $24.6 million from minority suppliers, $7.2 million of which was from African American suppliers. In fiscal year 2003, purchases from West Philadelphia suppliers amounted to $61.6 million, with purchases from minority suppliers totaling $41.4 million, $13.1 million from African American suppliers. And through a supplier mentoring program, we helped several small businesses acquire e-commerce capability, not just to enable them to serve us more effectively but also to make them more viable and competitive in the open market. That is exactly the kind of sustainable, inner-city small-business creation that Michael Porter talks about.

Of the $550 million in total construction projects funded since the inception of the Economic Opportunity Program, $134 million in funding (nearly a quarter of the total) has been committed to minority- and women-owned businesses. More recent Penn-sponsored construction at four sites awarded minority- and women-owned businesses

$45.5 million in contracts, between 22 and 25 percent of all the contracts awarded for these ventures.

Penn now employs more than three thousand West Philadelphia residents, which does not include the two-hundred-plus residents who work at the Inn at Penn, Sheraton University City Hotel, and the Penn Bookstore. Unique/Advantage, an African American women-owned firm, assists Penn by serving as the preferred placement agency. In 2003, Unique/Advantage placed 714 employees at Penn and the University of Pennsylvania hospital system; 174 of them were West Philadelphia residents. Many of Penn's vendors are growing to serve an expanding client base in the Philadelphia region.

All told, these two groups of interventions have played a substantial role in contributing to neighborhood revitalization. More than 150,000 square feet of new retail inventory was added and twenty-five new stores opened in the four-year period from 1999 to 2003 alone. The gross sales of added new retailers exceed $200 million annually. University City is now recognized as an attractive market for retailers, and 98 percent of Penn-owned retail inventory had been leased or committed as of early 2004. Penn encouraged the creation of thousands of new private-sector jobs for local residents. And the neighborhood's economic infrastructure is growing stronger and more stable through the Buy West Philadelphia and GPUAC initiatives.

Success, of course, does not come without some trials. We made mistakes along the way and we learned some lessons the hard way. Although it ultimately turned out well, the movie-theater debacle was especially painful while we were living through it. And we learned through the Fresh Grocer and garage construction that outsourcing management of real-estate development projects that used our capital was a costly mistake. In 1998, Penn had hired a nationally known property-management company to oversee our extensive real-estate holdings and be responsible for all construction management. It was heralded by the *Wall Street Journal* as "innovative"—the first arrangement of its kind between a university and a real-estate company. At one point, the company was managing $800 million worth of capital projects as well as overseeing more than twelve million square feet of Penn's property, considered the largest real-estate contract in the city. But this innovative relationship came to a crashing halt. In 2002 we both agreed it was time to unwind. We learned that for outsourcing on that scale to work, we had to have top-level, continuous, and intensive internal management.

And, in our painfully learned experience, a vast portfolio of mixed-use needs probably requires multiple outsourcing contracts. We enhanced Penn's facilities-management and real-estate management operations, with Omar Blaik in charge, and he hired a professional, experienced team. With another of John Wanamaker's memorable quotes resounding, it was time to "do the next thing." In 2003, Blaik contracted with Madison Marquette, a boutique retail adviser and broker based in Washington, D.C., to undertake a full mapping of retail needs and further opportunities for growth in University City. They began a remerchandising campaign for the new retail districts and assumed leasing responsibilities for Penn's rapidly expanding retail portfolio, which includes major retailers such as the Gap, Cosi, Barnes and Noble, the Bridge Cinema, Urban Outfitters, Ann Taylor Loft, Marathon Grill, and others. Penn's commercial and residential real estate portfolios are now managed, with professional internal oversight, by a variety of firms rather than one and are held to strict-bid and managed standards. Experienced private parties handle financing for, and construction management of, the development of noncampus buildings, again with relevant, professional Penn oversight. On-campus construction projects and facilities management are managed internally.

And despite the hard knocks, Penn's investment of about $170 million in Sansom Common and the 40th and Walnut streets ventures, while several million dollars over budget, had attracted approximately $370 million in private investment in West Philadelphia retail by 2004. Scores of new shops that run the gamut have opened throughout the neighborhood. Thousands of people—from the Penn community, from the neighborhood, from all over the region—are frequenting shops, restaurants, and cultural venues that came into being as a direct result of efforts to redevelop a dying commercial core into a thriving, productive asset. The crowds on the streets have made the neighborhood safer and much more exciting. It has been a shot in the arm for the local economy. It has made University City attractive to private developers. And it has made the neighborhood a more vibrant part of the life of the city.

CHAPTER 8

Investing in Public Education

ITS OFFICIAL NAME is the Sadie Tanner Mossell Alexander University of Pennsylvania Partnership School, but since opening in fall 2001, the innovative, state-of-the art, newest public school in Philadelphia has been known simply as Penn Alexander or, more affectionately, "the Sadie School." Situated on a Penn-owned, five-acre site bordered by 42nd and 43rd streets between Locust and Spruce, the $19 million, eighty-three-thousand-square-foot building was constructed with funds from the capital budget of the School District of Philadelphia. It houses students from pre-kindergarten through grade 8 in a welcoming environment with bright primary-color walls covered with student artwork. Twenty-eight classrooms with oversized windows are grouped around a three-story atrium that features a carpeted amphitheater and seating area. The school includes a gymnasium/auditorium, cafeteria, specialized art, music, and science facilities, and an instructional media center that combines a library, computer facility, and broadcast studio. Landscaped grounds provide students with a play field, rain garden, and outdoor science classroom.

Penn Alexander represents what was in many ways Penn's greatest gamble in West Philadelphia. I suppose that is why I have left this part of the story until last. The school experience highlights the range of partners as well as the breadth of intensely emotional arguments that revolve around the issue of education, from how best to serve our children to maintaining property values.

Good public-school options are crucial for the stability of residential neighborhoods. Families are attracted to and remain in neighborhoods with good schools. But, as Jane Jacobs observed, "good schools are impossible in any unstable neighborhood with high pupil turnover rates, and this includes unstable neighborhoods which also have good housing."[1] Like families everywhere, those in University City wanted better educational opportunities for their children, just as they wanted better opportunities for the neighborhood in general. The years of failing schools had contributed to declining real-estate values, abandoned housing, and increased crime. It stands to reason that neighborhoods with higher-quality schools and a broader range of school choice have a powerful competitive advantage over other communities. If families in University City had more favorable educational options, the neighborhood's stock could soar.

An urban university like Penn, with education as its core mission, has the potential to influence the quality of public education significantly. A substantial number of faculty and students have the expertise and/or the motivation to provide enriched educational opportunities for school-age children. It certainly can be a win-win situation when a university becomes engaged in the improvement of local public schools: the university supplements its academic curriculum by providing its own students with real-world experience, and the schoolchildren reap the tangible benefits. In the longer term, university engagement can constructively influence policies and programming and can contribute to a better understanding of options for improving the public education system. Many American colleges and universities have recognized this synergy and are active in a variety of ways in their local public schools.

The transformation of the schools in the neighborhood was one of Penn's goals from the start when planning the West Philadelphia Initiatives, but it would have been more difficult to effect this change had we failed to focus on the community's other needs. Through the clean and safe efforts, the housing-revitalization program, and retail and economic development, we were fostering relationships of greater trust among our neighbors: building social capital and developing a community of shared values. We could then call on this new social capital to do something substantial to improve the local schools.

There is no doubt that memories of my early years in the Philadelphia public schools influenced my personal stake. When West Philadelphia's Shaw Middle School chose to honor me in 1995, it was with particular pleasure that I returned to the scene of my middle-school years (somewhat anguished as they were) to be inducted into the Hall of Fame. Upon entering the school, I found a principal full of enthusiasm and energy, teachers who were obviously dedicated, and Penn students who were actively involved with the school through tutoring and mentoring programs. However, I could not help but observe how badly the building had deteriorated and the extent of the state of disrepair—structural and spiritual—of the Philadelphia public schools. The Hall of Fame event captured my attention, and as a result I spent a lot more time ruminating about public-school education in Philadelphia than I had ever anticipated. The problems of the Philadelphia public schools were dire indeed, with one-quarter of first-graders held back, 70 percent of elementary-school students reading below grade level, a failure rate of 49 percent among all ninth-graders, at least 30 percent of high-school students dropping out, and many graduates ill prepared for jobs or college.[2]

Like many urban school districts, Philadelphia's was burdened with problems—overcrowding, aging and dilapidated facilities, a lack of resources—that seemed insurmountable. State and city leaders clashed for years over ways to ease the district's considerable fiscal and academic woes. The state altered its funding formula for schools, and a freeze in the 1992–93 school year and then another in 1995 added to the turbulence in Philadelphia's schools. The number of poor and immigrant students in the city continued to grow, the tax base eroded, and some experts felt that the state support did not even keep pace with inflation. The district's huge budget cuts included librarians, music and art teachers, reading specialists, and classroom aides. Many of these reductions fell disproportionately on poor schools already overcrowded and in disrepair.

Then, in 1994, Pennsylvania Commonwealth Court Judge Doris Smith ruled on a school-desegregation suit that had been on the books since 1971. Finding rampant racial inequality in Philadelphia schools, Smith's ruling shifted the arena from desegregation to school reform. The issue became how to guarantee educational equity to poor and Hispanic and African American students who made up the overwhelming majority of students in the school system (in which only 23 percent of the students were white). Smith ordered a panel of national education experts to study the school district and formulate recommendations for reform. The resulting report painted a troubling picture of a dysfunctional system that had failed to educate the majority of its students effectively, especially those in the poorest neighborhoods. The panel concluded that the magnet schools, a centerpiece of the system's voluntary desegregation effort, were not available to enough minority students and enrolled a disproportionately high number of white students. Even as the panel acknowledged the need for the state to "change its inherently inequitable system for financing public education," it also found that district spending on administrative overhead was bloated, and that the way it distributed money shortchanged the racially isolated, poor schools. Gail Tomlinson of the Citizens Committee for Public Education in Philadelphia, a volunteer advocacy group, was quoted in the *Philadelphia Inquirer:* "Frankly, I think it's an indictment of us all that such a laundry list of problems in public education could be developed. . . . It's not just the money, the administration, not just the public. All of us have not done our best for the kids of this city."[3] Sweeping reforms recommended by the panel's report were intended to restructure the school system, topple the prejudice and indifference that pervaded the schools, and introduce accountability and new standards.

Meanwhile, Philadelphia's new superintendent of schools, historian-theologian-lawyer-turned-educator David Hornbeck, had been hired to implement his ten-point Children Achieving agenda, aimed at increasing student achievement across the district. Hornbeck, who had consulted on a number of successful school-reform efforts elsewhere, was a firm believer in the possibility of urban school reform. Many of the school panel's recommendations were in line with his own (some of which were already in motion), including reconstituting failing schools, school-based management, a greater level of community participation, more coordination with social-service agencies, full-day kindergarten, more extensive preschool, smaller class sizes in the lower grades, performance contracts for administrators and principals, and higher academic standards. A $50 million grant to the Philadelphia public schools from the Annenberg Challenge (the half-billion-dollar gift to American education from the Annenberg Foundation) supported the school-reform effort.[4]

All the recipients of Annenberg funds had to embody some critical components of the Challenge's philosophy: strong links with community organizations; collaborative networks of schools that crossed enduring political barricades; and a commitment to the idea that race, class, and other inequities must not keep a single child from high-quality teaching and learning. This philosophy was at the heart of the Challenge's insistence that the professional, political, labor, and business leadership in the regions submitting proposals commit to the substantial financial, political, and moral support needed to create a policy environment that clears the way for the redesign of its schools.[5] To that end, I joined the Board of Directors of Greater Philadelphia First (GPF) and served as a member of GPF's Philadelphia Public School/Business Partnership for Reform and its subcommittee that provided management oversight for the Annenberg grant and the $100 million in matching funds that were raised from business, foundation, and public donors.

The Hornbeck era was stormy, marked by continuing controversy and heated rhetoric. Almost from day one Hornbeck, who felt that seniority rules too often sheltered incompetent teachers, battled with the teachers union, especially over his call for more teacher accountability and performance-based pay. To some extent, this clash reflected the national debate over standards. Under Hornbeck, the entire Philadelphia school district was reorganized into twenty-two clusters of roughly eleven schools each, so that schools could organize their reform efforts within a smaller, more supportive structure (rather than dealing with the huge, bureaucratic downtown administration office), essentially breaking into "small learning communities." Some clusters fostered a common vision and common strategies across schools; others preferred to have each school or small learning community take the initiative. In West Philadelphia, for example, the cluster's primary professional-development emphasis was on team-building, creating small learning communities within larger schools, encouraging interdisciplinary teaching and cooperative learning, and using alternative assessments.

Restructuring the school district into clusters was not the only significant change. Adding fuel to the reform effort was Pennsylvania's charter-school law, Senate Bill 123, signed by then-governor Tom Ridge in 1997.[6] Charter schools are deregulated public schools that have far more flexibility than traditional public schools. Freed from many state and local regulations and rules, charters are nonetheless held accountable for improving student achievement.[7] Under the legislation, charters can be formed by teachers, parents, colleges and universities, museums, and a number of other entities. In Philadelphia, most charter schools accept students by a computerized lottery held before the school year begins. In the admissions process, the school accepts applications until a certain deadline. If by that deadline the school has more applications than spaces available, a computer system randomly selects the students who will attend. A charter school may focus on a new approach to curriculum and learning, a new organizational approach, or other features that set it apart from what a standard public school offers. Among the many and varied charter schools in Philadelphia are those that specialize in architecture and design, performing arts, computer or technical skills, math and science, maritime and naval careers, and entrepreneurship.

Despite these and other comprehensive reforms, such as the implementation of full-day kindergarten, improvements in reading, math, and science scores on standardized tests, and improved attendance, by 1998 Hornbeck was threatening to close the schools if the state did not increase funding. The next few years would see continuing controversy, such as the state Department of Education's $2.7 million, no-bid contract awarded to Edison Schools, Inc. (which would later take over management of a number of the city's schools), to analyze the Philadelphia school district. Then a contract dispute over Act 46, a state law passed in 2000, pitted the union and the school district against each other again, with the new legislation forbidding the teachers' old contract terms to be extended until a new one was in place. A teachers' strike, the first walkout in nearly twenty years, ended after one weekend without disrupting classrooms, but it highlighted the acrimony between the school district and the teachers. Act 46 also gave Governor Ridge broad powers to take over the school district if it failed to provide an adequate educational program. That is precisely what happened in 2001 with the stunning state takeover of the entire Philadelphia school system. Subsequent reform efforts resulted in the implementation of a variety of management approaches in different schools that included an increase in the number of magnet schools, conversion to charters, private management, and, as in the case of Penn, university partnership. Such was the dizzying state of affairs of the school district at the time Penn was working on its public-school initiatives.

Through the Graduate School of Education and the Center for Community Partnerships (CCP), the University was already deeply committed to improving the learning environment in schools throughout West Philadelphia, and a number of programs and projects were in progress. There had been collaborations with community and school leaders since the mid-1980s, and since its formal establishment in 1992, CCP had established a track record in academically based community service, direct traditional service, and community development. These efforts were real and substantial, although it had taken a long time to overthrow the yoke of suspicion and distrust that had lingered since the University City High School debacle in the 1970s. That is when Penn pulled its resources from the public-school initiative with which it had been involved to a limited degree, leaving many in the community enraged. In addition, a long-standing relationship with neighboring Henry Lea Elementary School had diminished somewhat, compounding the local population's skepticism about the University's motives. When Penn began to lead the move for a new school, there was understandably resistance from many who feared its involvement would, once again, be transitory.

Kate Ward Gaus, who was part of the parents' governance council at the Powell School (a local elementary school) during the mid-1980s, recalls the skepticism many families had about Penn. "Several faculty members and many families had transferred from the Lea School, which had benefited from Penn affiliation and support in the previous decade. But when the dynamics of the Lea School shifted, in part because of a change in leadership that wasn't receptive to the University's involvement, many felt abandoned by what they perceived as Penn's decision to decrease its presence."[8] By the time Gaus's children entered Powell, the school was considered "the only viable option" in the neighborhood, according to Gaus. It was also the only one of the neighborhood schools with a white presence. The Lea School, housed in a hundred-year-old building, was in steep decline.

In recent years, Penn had attracted significant grant funds that went directly to benefit West Philadelphia public schools, but the University's commitment went far beyond funding programs. Urban studies professor Ira Harkavy, CCP's director, and Graduate School of Education dean Susan Fuhrman agreed to head two of the school district's local "cluster resource boards," which included a broad range of business, institutional, and civic leaders. Harkavy led the resource board that represented University City High School and its "feeder" schools, while Fuhrman led the West Philadelphia Cluster Resource Board, representing West Philadelphia High School and its "feeder" schools.

Much though the University had worked to improve the learning environment in a number of local schools, we still had to face some hard facts. Children from low-income families by and large were trapped in these struggling schools. Their parents had little choice and even less hope of seeing their children receive a good education. Middle-class families with school-age children in University City did have a choice: they could send their children to a private school downtown or in the suburbs—an option a number of people had already taken—or they could pick up and move to the suburbs. What was it going to take to give children from impoverished families a reason to hope and middle-class families a reason to stay and become truly vested in the neighborhood? The answer would become clear to a large number of stakeholders: an excellent new school.

The question remained: what kind of school?

The 1993 Penn Faculty and Staff for Neighborhood Issues (PFSNI) report and the 1995 Spruce Hill Community Renewal Plan (mentioned in earlier chapters) had recommended a new school to serve University City as well as to help relieve overcrowding in surrounding schools.[9] Thus began the first of many debates. Some wanted a charter school. Others lobbied for a magnet school. Many argued for a private lab school. The general feeling was it should be anything but a University-assisted neighborhood public school, because there was no way one could ever get the school district and the teachers union to agree on much of anything, let alone a formula for running such a school, so contentious was the relationship between the two.

In the early stages, Penn sought to work with a neighboring private school in hopes of creating a neighborhood public school, and the initial reactions were promising. Board members of the private University City New School, of which Penn was a longtime landlord and patron, were enthusiastic. They felt that a modest boost to their enrollment would stabilize the school, and they were excited about having Penn's assistance in executing this conversion. A number of Penn faculty members living in West Philadelphia were also enthusiastic. This would be a school where they could send their children without any reservations. In effect, they were saying, "Build this school, and not only will we stay, more of our colleagues will come to live in University City."

Better yet, some suggested, if the University wanted the ultimate faculty recruitment and retention tool, why not have Penn launch and run its own private school, free from all regulatory constraints and political hassles? Were these tempting options for Penn to consider? Viewed narrowly in the context of some immediate institutional objectives, the answer was yes. This would be a great boon to faculty recruitment and a wonderful laboratory for the Graduate School of

Education. Columbia had just announced it was building a private school for faculty children.

However, through the lens of community-development efforts, there were major flaws with both options. The biggest flaw in the option of converting the private school into a neighborhood school was a relatively low enrollment figure—on the order of two hundred students. The school's board members were concerned that boosting enrollment beyond that range would translate into larger class sizes and new students who would radically alter the character of the school. But in fact, what was needed was precisely a school that was more diverse and representative of the local area.

We wanted a neighborhood school in the fullest sense, one that would express the shared values of community that Penn was trying to embody. A school enrolling a relatively small and select group of students would not meet that standard. We had the same reservations about a private school. If we sought to be *of* as well as *in* the community, creating a private school for the children of our faculty and staff undermined that message and philosophy. Finally, at the school district's urging, we did explore the idea of creating a magnet school that would draw children from all over the city, but again, that prospect clashed with the goal of creating a school that was *in* and *for* the neighborhood.

We chose to aim high. Susan Fuhrman, dean of the Graduate School of Education, and Steve Schutt, my chief of staff, led the charge to build a Penn-assisted, inclusive neighborhood public school whose enrollment would reflect the broad diversity of University City. Only a goal of this magnitude would capture the public's imagination and send the strongest possible signal to our neighbors that Penn was deeply committed to a sustainable future for University City. However, for this public school to be a model of best practices and innovations to benefit the neighboring schools and ultimately urban public education, we had to find a way to involve the School District of Philadelphia and the Philadelphia Federation of Teachers (PFT) in a true partnership. We believed that nothing short of a three-way partnership would do.

The task was daunting: the school district and teachers union were at each other's throats, each too protective of its respective turf. Tensions between the two sides were very real and palpable. Steve Schutt acted as liaison, working tirelessly to bring the school district and the teachers union together and to broker the deal. Steve had been Senator Harris Wofford's chief of staff and knew the players well. Although I met with PFT president Ted Kirsch and Superintendent Hornbeck several times, it was Schutt who attended countless meetings, many on a one-to-one basis, behind closed doors with Penn alumnus Pedro Ramos, Philadelphia School Board president, Germaine Ingram of the school district, or PFT president Ted Kirsch and Jerry Jordan, also of the PFT. We made a judgment call to conduct these conversations and negotiations with the school district and the teachers union in confidence, out of the public's eye. It was important not only to present this as a solid partnership but also to be absolutely certain that such a partnership was indeed established before we announced it. Little did we guess how this decision would come back to haunt us.

What kept people at the table was the notion that the new school could serve as a demonstration site for teachers and a catalyst for academic development for all the public schools in the community, and ultimately throughout the district. To their great credit, there was a genuine desire both by the school district and by the teachers union to accomplish something of lasting value to the schoolchildren and to public education, and neither side wanted to be perceived as an enemy of progress. Moreover, both sides viewed the prospect of a historic partnership with Penn through the prism of enlightened self-interest. For the school district, this offered an opportunity to extend the boundaries of experimentation to new kinds of partnerships with higher education. If it worked, there were many other colleges and universities in Philadelphia who might be called upon to step up their involvement. The timing could not have been better: with a new school superintendent as well as a new school board president, the Penn-assisted school offered the prospect of legitimacy and optimism for the school-reform efforts. It was not surprising that Hornbeck and Ramos expressed immediate interest in the idea.

For the PFT, this was an opportunity not only to prove that additional resources and extra dollars for smaller classrooms produced better results but also to show the world that teachers unions were not reactionaries who opposed any innovation that threatened the status quo, regardless of its impact on children. The challenge was to have all the stakeholders on the same page while satisfying their individual interests as well. PFT's Kirsch quickly embraced the opportunity to forge an agreement that would energize teachers and benefit schoolchildren. The PFT showed real flexibility in agreeing to site selection for the new school and to continuing Penn involvement, which would prove to be a critical component in fostering an innovative and unified teaching culture in the school.

It took a year to hammer out the details and the many compromises, a feat that seemed altogether unlikely, and we managed to keep negotiations quiet. In June 1998, as we were ironing out the last details of the memorandum of understanding, we learned of a leak to a local newspaper, which was planning to announce the partnership the very next day. Although we were not quite ready to go public, we were forced to scurry to preempt the media. Despite our best efforts at keeping lines of communication open with the various stakeholders as we pursued the West Philadelphia Initiatives, this particular agreement had been done behind closed doors because of the delicacy of the negotiations. Yet the last thing we wanted was to alienate the very community with which we were working so hard to forge a relationship. As one might expect, the announcement of the fait accompli was met with harsh criticism by some who felt left out of the decision-making process. Despite this setback, having the memorandum of understanding in hand assured a more solid foundation for building community support.

The memorandum of understanding formalized an agreement that had been reached regarding three key issues: (1) to develop a new public school; (2) to limit enrollment to children living in a designated catchment area (instead of enrolling students through a citywide lottery); and

(3) to use school-district capital funds for construction but have Penn select the architect and manage the project. The school district determined the boundaries for the school's catchment area, with the goal of achieving a diverse student body based on neighborhood demographics. Acknowledging an additional obligation to existing local schools, Penn agreed to leverage its resources to improve other neighborhood public schools as well. In addition, we made a separate multi-year commitment of support to the nearby Henry Lea elementary school. We agreed to provide $1.5 million for the school over the next three years to lower its class sizes. Graduate School of Education faculty and students would help strengthen Lea's curriculum in math, science, and reading. Penn would support a librarian for three years and help the district raise funds for equipment and books in a new library that the district would build at Lea. And we agreed to stay at Lea as a long-term partner.

Under the terms of the memorandum of understanding, the University agreed to lease land to the School District of Philadelphia for $1 per year and to provide up to $700,000 in annual operating support for ten years (based on an allocation of $1,000 per student), in order to augment the district's support. This would allow the new Penn-assisted school to have smaller classes and provide other, research-driven "best practices" in the curriculum. Penn would offer academic support through the University's Graduate School of Education. The school district agreed to work with the University on the design and construction of the school. Although responsibility for supervising construction was a contentious issue, we were able to establish a "turn-key" agreement. The school district would provide capital funding, but the school would be paid for up-front by Penn, which would then turn over the key to the school district after completion of the building and payment by the School District of Philadelphia. We supplemented funds from the district with additional resources provided by several Penn donors who were captivated by the project.

The school district agreed to establish a curriculum that would meet or exceed high district standards and to allow Penn to work with its leadership on the selection of a principal and faculty. The district had been advocating that the state provide additional operating funding and was eager to demonstrate that it was seeking every available opportunity to leverage local resources. The PFT agreed to make the new school a demonstration school. It would provide rigorous training that focused on the professional growth and development of teachers, first from other West Philadelphia schools and eventually throughout the city. Perhaps even more significant, PFT agreed to support the selection of teachers based on classroom demonstrations and written and oral examinations rather than seniority. This was a first, and a marked change from the status quo. The PFT viewed the many opportunities for both the children and the teachers as worthy of circumventing union rules. It recognized the benefit of linking the union with a progressive education initiative. PFT president Kirsch said, in commenting on the plan, that the partnership represented a unique opportunity for the federation and its members to participate in designing a school and a curriculum from the ground up.

However, this school had to be more than the best school in theory. It had to work. It had to capture the community's energy and the public's imagination and support. It had to have an innovative curriculum and teaching strategies based on the best educational research. It had to be located in the heart of the neighborhood. Its building design needed to promote learning, public access, and civic engagement.

Because it was linked to ongoing neighborhood revitalization, the new public school also needed to serve as a community center that offered many options: a variety of vocational, recreational, and adult-education programs; academic enrichment for students and professional-development activities for teachers; cultural events; and a town hall where the community could come together to explore and debate issues and visions of the future. In many ways, the school would be modeled in the vein of the community-school movement that gained national visibility in the 1930s, fueled by the Charles Stewart Mott Foundation and its work in Flint, Michigan. Much like those community schools, the new school would foster strong partnerships, build the community's strengths and embrace its diversity, and encourage a culture of lifelong learning.

The most practical location for the new building was the same site on which the University City New School stood. Penn had provided the building since 1973 and had kept the rent quite reasonable, often forgiving it during periods of crisis. To make room for the Penn-assisted school, the UC New School would have to relocate, as would the Parent Infant Center and the University-owned Penn Children's Center. Penn promised to help these institutions find new homes with university support for relocation expenses. Ultimately, several UC New School staffers, including Elizabeth A. Retay, head of the school, participated in the yearlong planning for the new public school.

Once the PFT and district partnership was established and set the parameters for the school's development, we embarked on a community-wide planning process. First and foremost, everything about the school—from the design of the curriculum to the design of the building to its emergence as a neighborhood hub for community learning and enrichment—needed to be *of* the neighborhood. That meant many stakeholders had to be involved in creating, refining, and executing a shared vision for all this school could be. Mechanisms were established to allow for shared ownership of the process, including the formation of three separate committees: Educational Programming, Site and Facility, and Community Programming. Each committee was made up of Penn faculty and administrators, neighborhood residents, teachers, and clergy, civic activists and arts advocates, and child-care professionals.

The Educational Programming Committee, chaired by Nancy Streim, associate dean of the Graduate School of Education, drew on the varied expertise and multiple perspectives of its members to develop a clear pedagogical framework in which the GSE would work with the principal and teachers to design a rich curriculum, a culture for professional development for in-service teachers, and a host of best practices.

The Site and Facility Committee, chaired by Tom Lussenhop of the Office of Real Estate and Planning and Ted Skierski of the School District of Philadelphia, took pains to ensure that the school building and school grounds were the best fit for the neighborhood. In other words, beautiful but not ornate, functional and flexible but not extravagant, and open and accessible, while protecting the needs of the children.

The Community Programming Committee was chaired by Kate Ward Gaus on Penn's staff and Larry Bell, executive director of West Philadelphia Partnership. The committee offered a vision of a community school that would enhance the quality of life for everyone in the neighborhood. The committee saw the school offering cooking classes, music instruction, and counseling, forums on civic issues, recreational activities, parent-child learning activities, technology training, concerts, and shows. The list was both amazingly creative and nearly endless.

These three committees took nine months to produce a framework that would be ready for prime time in the fall of 1999. They made site visits to schools within the school district as well as to some in Boston and New York City. They spoke with education practitioners and researchers. They tried to address every conceivable aspect of the school: curriculum, community outreach, and construction. They were certain that their neighbors would cheer this project, because, after all, what was not to like?

As we would soon find out, there was at least one complaint for just about everything.

We finished planning in 1999, but it would be another two years before we broke ground. First, we discovered that, particularly when it comes to schools, bitter memories and resentments do not go gently into the night. Despite all the progress we had made—and despite very inclusive and very public deliberations each step of the way—some in the neighborhood wondered aloud whether Penn's proposal was a ploy to create a school just for the children of our own affiliates. Others, including several elected officials, argued strenuously that if Penn was willing to invest heavily in a neighborhood school, we should direct our time and resources exclusively toward an existing school that desperately needed renovations, repairs, and resources. Others wanted the new school to be a magnet school, open to all the children of Philadelphia.

Yet, differing opinions aside, nobody doubted that a Penn-assisted school would be wonderful. And that would prove to be the biggest part of the problem. The prospect of a Penn-assisted school nearby raised concerns that the neighborhood would divide into "haves" and "have-nots." Children who got to attend the new school would enjoy all the advantages of the haves. The children who were left behind in old schools were doomed to suffer the deprivations of the have-nots. Understandably, emotions ran high. The air of mistrust and skepticism made the task more challenging for Fuhrman, Schutt, and Lucy Kerman, special projects coordinator in my office, and others as they continued to exert indefatigable efforts to build support for the new school. In fact, the catchment area would become the most contentious issue.

Some at Penn argued that the risks of moving forward on the school were too great, and they counseled us to scratch the idea altogether. We felt passionately, however, that a strong neighborhood public school would prove to be the most important element in redeveloping the community and building sustainability. To continue moving forward, we held the first of what would become several town meetings with neighbors, community leaders, and elected officials, including representatives of the school district and the teachers union. As might be imagined, these meetings were often quite heated. It was not easy listening to some of the fiery rhetoric about big bad Penn.

I will never forget one particularly difficult meeting. As cochairwoman of newly elected mayor John Street's transition team, I attended some of the town meetings that the mayor held throughout the city right after his election. When he scheduled a meeting in West Philadelphia to talk about schooling, I offered to join him. The mayor began by announcing that he was delighted to have me there, especially since I was a product of the public schools in West Philadelphia and, he continued, Penn was now involved in a potentially transformational experiment in public education. He had not anticipated the audience's negative response. Some were quite vocal in their feelings about Penn, arguing that nothing Penn had ever done for the schools in West Philadelphia had ever worked, that we thought we were such do-gooders but only did what we wanted to; "what about what the children really need and what about getting the parents more involved?" I was horrified by the venomous reaction from some people. Even though we thought we had done everything we could to involve just about everyone in the community, it was quite a chilling experience and highlighted just how difficult a project this was.

We were not concerned about the cynics and hecklers but did worry about the families whose concerns were legitimate. They argued vociferously that Penn needed to serve the entire community, not just families who lived in the catchment area, whatever that would turn out to be. They were worried that if Penn poured resources into this new school, other West Philadelphia elementary schools, such as Powell, Lea, Drew, and Wilson, would suffer from a loss of both financial and human capital.

Community members found themselves taking sides. Some supported a neighborhood catchment area and others wanted a larger "attendance by lottery" magnet school available to the whole city. No topic was more charged than that of the catchment area, and conversations about it could be overheard everywhere. There were all kinds of meetings, many in private homes with just a small group of residents, some of them held in secrecy. Even the neighborhood associations were pitted against each other over the catchment-area issue. One association, Spruce Hill, dropped out of the University City Community Council, which was in favor of the lottery plan. Sometimes the educational issues got lost in the clamor, and the conflict occasionally seemed to be more about who would benefit financially from the inevitable rise in property values in the catchment area than about who would benefit educationally.

Penn did not favor a lottery; neither did Mayor Street nor several school board members, who spoke out against it, saying a lottery would open the door to abuse. We were committed to the idea of a neighborhood school. How could it be a true neighborhood school if one child attended and his or her friend next door could not? But the prospect of getting unified support from the community looked increasingly dim. Some joked that it would be easier to build a prison in University City.

While it was up to the school board to determine the boundaries for the catchment area, Penn did have some input. Our prime concern was that the catchment area should reflect the diversity—racial, cultural, and economic—of the West Philadelphia community. To its credit, the school board strove to turn the hearings on the catchment issue into conversations, even reconfiguring the hearing room into a more inclusive space, with chairs set up in a square rather than in rows. There was a great deal of speculation and misinformation flying about. It took many months of wrangling and negotiation among community groups, Penn officials, and the school district to settle on an attendance zone that reflected the goal of diversity.

Ultimately, the catchment area was defined as an area roughly encompassing 40th to 47th streets from Sansom Street to Woodland Avenue. Announcing the forthcoming plans of the Board of Education to vote on the catchment area, the *Philadelphia Inquirer* reported on July 21, 2000,[10] that the racial composition of children aged five to thirteen in the attendance zone was 55.9 percent African American, 18.3 percent white, 19.8 percent Asian, 5 percent Hispanic, and 1 percent Native American. The area had a median household income falling just under $25,000, according to district data. The school board had met our criterion of diversity, and the establishment of the catchment area would move more than two hundred students from the Henry Lea School to the Penn-assisted school, greatly relieving the overcrowding at Lea. In addition, more than fifty children from the Wilson School and smaller numbers from the Drew and Powell schools would attend the new school.

The Penn-assisted school opened in fall 2001 with kindergarten and first grade. Because the new building was not ready, the school opened in existing space on the site. After construction was completed in 2002, Head Start and grades 2, 5, and 6 were added. Successive grades were filled in the next two years, and full enrollment from prekindergarten to eighth grade was achieved by 2004, providing a new middle-school option. It is a thrill to walk the halls today and see the diverse student body, representing some nineteen countries. These children are receiving an education in a learning environment that is tailored to each child's strengths and challenges. All classrooms are bright and big-windowed, their design based on data showing that students perform better when they learn in rooms with windows and natural light.[11] Classes are small and manageable, reflecting research that links class size to students' academic success.[12] The student-teacher ratio is seventeen to one in kindergarten and twenty-three to one in first through eighth grades. The school's "buddy system" has fifth- and sixth-graders serving as mentors to the younger children, reading and sharing stories with them about twice a week.

Children at Penn Alexander have classes in music, art, physical education, technology, and Spanish. Penn Alexander is the only elementary school in the district to provide all of these subjects under one roof. Thanks to a state Department of Environmental Protection Growing Greener Grant, an innovative storm-water management project on the grounds of the school serves as a natural classroom. Here, the topography is not a re-creation. It is the original landscape, with the rain garden located at the bottom of the hill down which the water has long flowed. A platform overlooks the rain garden, where the children can observe, draw, and learn. The school worked with Penn's Graduate School of Education and the Philadelphia Water Department to develop curriculum materials, enabling kindergarteners through eighth-graders to take advantage of what can be learned from the site.

Penn's associate dean of the Graduate School of Education provides ongoing assistance with all aspects of school development. GSE faculty members guide the selection of best curricula, coteach classes, mentor individual teachers, develop special curriculum projects with teachers and students, and conduct training workshops. Penn academic departments, health-sciences schools, museum, bookstore, Annenberg Center, and community-service organizations offer special programs for students. Penn students provide tutoring assistance in math, reading, and English language. Student teachers from the GSE are assigned to the school.

The school's student body continues to reflect the diversity of the surrounding community: 57 percent African American, 19 percent Caucasian, 18 percent Asian, and 6 percent Latino. International students represent 25 percent of the student body, and students from Penn-affiliated families (staff, faculty, students) represent 23 percent of the enrollment. Class size remains substantially lower than the citywide average.

And the students are thriving. At least 70 percent of primary-grade students demonstrate proficiency in reading and math on standardized tests. In the *Inquirer's Report Card on the Schools*, Penn Alexander's third-graders placed in the top 20 percent of schools statewide for reading and math scores on the mandatory state assessment tests.[13] All students are required to read for thirty minutes each night, and the school stresses parental involvement, asking parents to volunteer their time and unique skills and to chaperone school events. More than 25 percent of students participate in the school's music program, receiving individual instruction on string, wind, brass, and percussion instruments; all students enjoy a yearlong concert series featuring jazz and classical musicians from Penn.

The school has already been associated with an impressive list of awards and intellectual achievements. In 2004, the Knowledge Works Foundation, an Ohio-based nonprofit focusing on educational philanthropy, awarded the Penn Alexander School placement in the Schools as Centers of Community Honors Society. The foundation was particularly impressed by the unique partnership of the school and the University. A Head Start teacher from the school was recognized by the school district as Outstanding Early Educator of the Year for 2003–04. Teachers from the school have presented papers at major professional meetings, including the National Council of Teachers of Mathematics, International Reading Association, National Association for the Education of Young Children, and National Writing Project. Perhaps most rewarding is the fact that at the Carver Science Fair (the largest public-private science fair in the country), sixth- and seventh-graders from the school have taken four first-place awards, one second-place award, and numerous honorable mentions. And equally exciting, nine second-grade students have had their poetry published in the *Young American Poetry Digest*. It is no wonder that the ratio of applicants to teaching positions at the school is approximately twenty-five to one.

The Penn Alexander School reflects the inclusive spirit of partnership between the University of Pennsylvania and the neighborhood, right down to its name: Sadie Alexander was the first African American to earn a doctorate in economics at Penn (in 1921), as well as the first African American woman to earn a Penn law degree (in 1927) and practice law in Pennsylvania. Her struggle against segregation and discrimination in Philadelphia changed the course of history in the city and presaged the national civil-rights movement.

More work was needed to fulfill Penn's commitment to the other public schools in West Philadelphia. Penn participated actively, through the Graduate School of Education and the Center for Community Partnerships, in the efforts of the Philadelphia School Reform Commission to improve student performance in the lowest-performing schools in the city, several of which were in West Philadelphia. After the state took over the management of the schools, the district invited seven entities (some private-education companies like Edison and some not-for-profit institutions like Penn) to serve as educational-management organizations for a total of forty-five elementary and middle schools that registered the weakest performance on state assessment instruments.

For its schools, Penn focused on professional and leadership development, curriculum and assessment tools, and the school climate, providing technical assistance, resources, and management. For example, in work at three elementary schools, the Henry Lea School, William Bryant School, and Alexander Wilson School (the Partnership Schools), Penn provides intensive technical assistance and advice to each school's administration and teachers to improve student achievement in literacy, math, and science. With its partners, Penn has developed a professional-development model for staff, and it administers regular student assessments and monitors performance benchmarks. With additional grant support, a focused professional-development program in math and technology was developed through a "bridging" approach that includes teachers from both the Penn Alexander School and the Partnership Schools. Parent workshops encourage greater family involvement in the schools, and there is support for the development of a strong Home and School Association.

Penn also stepped up its involvement in all the middle schools and high schools in West Philadelphia (Figure 11). More than a hundred students annually are placed in the America Reads*America Counts federal work-study program to employ college students to help improve public-school students' literacy and math skills. Penn faculty and Center for Community Partnerships staff members orient and train students for the program. The Graduate School of Education provides professional-development training for all teachers and technical assistance and advice to school administrators. Curricular innovations are regularly tested and evaluated.

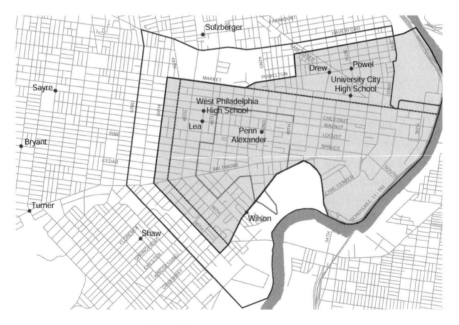

Figure 11
Locations of Penn Education Activities. John Kromer and Lucy Kerman, *West Philadelphia Initiatives: A Case Study in Urban Revitalization* (Philadelphia: University of Pennsylvania, 2004), p. 45.

Under the leadership of the Center for Community Partnerships, Penn faculty have developed more than ninety academic service-learning courses, most of which bring Penn students to work with West Philadelphia public-school students. These are academically rigorous courses based in traditional academic disciplines, but they add a service-learning component so that undergraduates can see, firsthand, the potential application of the disciplines they are studying.

Two of the longest-running courses serve as examples. In Robert Giegengack's urban-geology course, undergraduates learn, among other things, about lead poisoning and sources of lead exposure. In the service-learning component of the course, they work with local middle-school students to teach them where lead exposure in their homes might come from and how to mitigate risk of it. The youngsters then go out into the community, house to house, with Penn students to do volunteer environmental assessments. A second course, Nutrition, taught by anthropology professor Francis Johnston, focuses its service-learning component on educating inner-city children early about food and nutrition. The project (the Urban Nutrition Initiative, or UNI) has grown so dramatically over the years of the course that it now employs more than a hundred local high-school students during the summer and has a full-time director who was once a Penn student taking the course. The teens grow and tend urban vegetable gardens and run fresh-vegetable stands in and around neighborhood schools. All year long, with Penn undergraduates from the course, the local young growers take what they learn in the garden to local shelters, churches, and after-school programs at public schools, where they teach nutrition and healthy-cooking classes to children. As is clear in both of these courses, and the others like them, the schoolchildren and the Penn students themselves become problem solvers and educators.

Penn has also been developing evening and weekend community courses in all West Philadelphia schools, offering, at no charge, a wide range of academic, cultural, and recreational classes to all the youth and adults of West Philadelphia. It is especially gratifying to see how often teenagers and parents attend these classes together. And Penn students, staff, and faculty are still abundantly volunteering their time, energy, and creativity in these schools as tutors and mentors. The independent student newspaper, the *Daily Pennsylvanian*, now advises Shaw Middle School students on their own school paper, including writing, editing, layout, and photography. Watching our hardened editors' and reporters' pride at the work of their young students is a compelling tribute to the power of partnership.

Penn's impact on these West Philadelphia Partnership Schools has been substantial. Penn's university-assisted community schools program won the inaugural 2003 William T. Grant Foundation Youth Development Prize; the program was selected for the prize by the National Academy of Sciences from among nearly three hundred applications. Penn was designated number one in service-learning in *U.S. News and World Report*'s 2003 edition of *America's Best Colleges*. In 2000 Drew Elementary (kindergarten through eighth grade) was the most improved school in reading statewide. University City High School students working with the Center for Community Partnerships' Urban Nutrition Initiative have a higher attendance rate than their fellow students and students citywide, at 87 percent (compared to 75 percent schoolwide and just 55 percent districtwide); they also score at proficient levels, and all but two members of the 2003 senior-class cohort went on to postsecondary education. Additionally, UNI was cited as one of the four most promising school-based health and nutrition programs nationally in *Healthy Schools for Healthy Kids*, a major report published by the Robert Wood Johnson Foundation.[14] The Center's Community Arts Partnerships program has reintroduced the arts into all the local schools that had previously lacked instruction in music and fine arts.

One element of the memoradum of understanding remained unfulfilled—the agreement to relocate the overcrowded George Washington Carver High School for Engineering and Science from North Philadelphia to West Philadelphia. At the time, it seemed like a terrific plan. Carver would be in the midst of a technology corridor with Drexel

Education Initiatives Results

Since the opening of the Penn Alexander School in 2001, the school has already become well established as a community learning center and neighborhood resource.

+ The student body reflects the rich diversity of the surrounding community: 57 percent African American, 19 percent Caucasian, 18 percent Asian, and 6 percent Latino. International students represent 25 percent of the student body, and students from Penn-affiliated families (staff, faculty, students) represent 23 percent of enrollment.

+ Class size is substantially lower than the citywide average, with a maximum of seventeen students in kindergarten and twenty-three students in grades 1 to 8, supported by Penn's operating subsidy.

+ School architects Atkin, Olshin, Lawson-Bell and Associates received a Design Excellence award from the Philadelphia chapter of the American Institute of Architecture for the school's design.

+ The school received the 2004 Schuylkill Action Network Source Water Protection Award for its underground-water retention system.

+ At least 70 percent of primary-grade students demonstrate proficiency in reading and math on standardized tests.

+ The School District of Philadelphia recognized one of the Head Start (prekindergarten) teachers from the school as Outstanding Early Educator of the Year for 2003–04.

+ Teachers for the school have presented papers at major professional meetings, including the National Council of Teachers of Mathematics, International Reading Association, National Association for the Education of Young Children, and National Writing Project.

+ At the Carver Science Fair (the largest public-private science fair in the country) in the years 2002–03 and 2003–04, sixth- and seventh-graders from the school took four first-place awards, one second-place award, and numerous honorable mentions.

+ The music program includes individual instruction on string, wind, brass, and percussion instruments, as well as a year-long concert series featuring jazz and classical musicians from Penn. More than 25 percent of the students studied musical instruments at school in 2003.

+ Nine second-grade students have had their poetry published in the *Young American Poetry Digest.*

+ Every semester, ten Penn preprofessional students from the Graduate School of Education and two School of Social Work interns are placed at the school for practicums.

+ The ratio of teacher applicants to teaching positions at the school is approximately 25:1.

+ The school has an active community school two evenings a week, featuring educational, recreational, and cultural programming for adults and children from the neighborhood.

Penn's impact on other West Philadelphia public schools has also been substantial.

+ Selected by the National Academy of Sciences from nearly three hundred applications, Penn's University-Assisted Community School program won the inaugural 2003 William T. Grant Foundation Youth Development Prize.

+ Penn ranked no. 1 in service learning in *U.S. News and World Report*'s 2003 edition of *America's Best Colleges*.

+ Drew Elementary (K–8) was the most improved school in reading statewide in 2000.

+ University City High School students working with the Center for Community Partnership's Urban Nutrition Initiative have the highest attendance rate, at 87 percent (75 percent schoolwide, 55 percent districtwide). These students are scoring at proficient levels, and all but two members of the 2003 senior class cohort went on to postsecondary education.

+ The Center's Urban Nutrition Initiative was cited as one of the four most promising school-based health and nutrition programs nationally in *Healthy Schools for Healthy Kids*, a major report published by the Robert Wood Johnson Foundation in 2003. In the foundation's research on hundreds of programs studied in connection with the publication, UNI was one of four programs identified as the most promising models.

+ The Center's Community Arts Partnerships program has reintroduced the arts into local schools that had previously lacked instruction in music and fine arts.

Source: John Kromer and Lucy Kerman, *West Philadelphia Initiatives: A Case Study in Urban Revitalization* (Philadelphia: University of Pennsylvania, 2004), pp. 48–49.

University, Penn, and the University City Science Center. We agreed to find a site for the new school and proposed a spot near the 44th and Market streets elevated train stop, which pleased the parents. The school district rejected that idea, insisting that the high school be located closer to Penn. We settled on a plan for the city to pay the costs of constructing a new building for the magnet school, and the University, in partnership with the University City Science Center, agreed to provide the land at 38th and Market streets at a nominal cost.

The agreement, however, was not ideal from anyone's perspective. First, the land was not ours to give. It would utilize a large piece of property that might be invaluable for later development of the Science Center. Second, the site was diagonally across the street from University City High School, and we envisioned turf wars between the kids from the two very disparate types of schools. In 2002, the negotiations with the Science Center to acquire the land broke down as costs for the project escalated. By then, Paul Vallas had taken over leadership of the school district, making sweeping districtwide reforms in an effort to duplicate his success with Chicago's public-school system. It was decided to keep Carver in North Philadelphia, close to its core student population.

Despite some setbacks, Penn is helping to improve public education in West Philadelphia (see box for results). Moreover, the Penn Alexander School and the other public-school initiatives have energized Penn faculty, inspired its students, enlivened the neighborhood, and united neighborhood residents in improving their children's futures. And as I write, plans for two small new magnet high schools are being developed for University City, a significantly better outcome than moving Carver would have been. If all goes according to plan, they will share a site. One school will focus on the study of international cultures and languages and the other on technology. There are great hopes for public education in the West Philadelphia community.

CHAPTER 9

Civic Leadership

OVER THE NEXT DECADE, Penn will be spearheading its growth and development primarily eastward to the Schuylkill River, fulfilling the promise never again to encroach on the neighborhoods to the west, despite the fact that land there would be less expensive to assemble. Surface parking lots will be turned into student housing and recreational space. Abandoned industrial and commercial buildings will be converted into mixed-use facilities for teaching, scientific research, and technology-transfer enterprises. Shops, green spaces, and streets will connect University City to Center City.

These changes will occur because Penn, in shifting its perspective and development aspirations, linked all of its campus planning to its neighborhood-redevelopment strategies. No land acquisition was made, no renovation undertaken, no new building begun, without asking how it would affect the neighborhood and the city. Guided by a master plan developed in collaboration with the Olin Partnership, distinguished urban and landscape planners, we reexamined the campus fabric, including buildings, grounds, streets, and infrastructure, and took a hard, self-critical look at Penn's context within the city of Philadelphia. The selection of Laurie Olin as master planner was extremely important. Although his work and reputation were international in scope, he was both a Penn faculty member and had lived in the University City community for years. His commitment to the campus and the neighborhood greatly enriched the work.

The values that underpinned the plan we developed in 2001 included connectivity of the University with the neighborhood and the city, celebration of our historical heritage within Philadelphia, and development of community-friendly open space wherever possible. From these values, six goals emerged as key to achieving Penn's aspiration to become a great urban university connected to its neighborhood and the city. These included: (1) strengthening the connections of campus areas to each other and to the historic pedestrian core, while providing each area with revitalized open space to improve connection and invite the city in; (2) extending the quality, character, and amenities of the pedestrian core to all new development while (3) reinforcing the historic core as the center of campus life and learning; (4) engaging in historic preservation of buildings of significant character and value while attempting reintegration of existing structures into the urban fabric and constructing new contemporary-style buildings that embrace city streets and sidewalks; (5) continuing to enhance the neighborhood with good architecture and inviting public spaces that link and intertwine Penn and the community; and (6) connecting Penn to Center City with new continuous urban spaces and buildings.

We saw that we could promote connectivity with the community and the city by taking walls and fences down and emphasizing visual transparency of buildings and accessibility to open spaces. When the master plan was approved by the Board of Trustees we produced a twenty-minute video on our Web site that described the overall plan and proposed projects. People were actually taken aback by the open communication and lack of secrecy. As the work got under way, we validated each new building's massing and setbacks as they would affect the public realm. While we were renovating buildings we gave them new public entrances from the street side of campus as well as from internal courtyards. We re-clad buildings that had stern brick walls facing the street with new window and wall systems that improved their aesthetics and transparency. All along the south side of Walnut Street from 34th to 38th streets these efforts were transformative. The Van Pelt Library, the old Faculty Club, the Annenberg School for Communications, and the Graduate School of Education all had exciting and inviting new facades. The old Faculty Club, a seldom used facility with an imposing, unattractive brick facade, has been transformed into a completely window-clad home for the Art Department of Penn Design. It is now called the Charles Addams Fine Arts Hall, after the *New Yorker* cartoonist and Penn alum. Here we might have been a bit carried away with the idea of transparency; the nude models posing for art students began to create quite a buzz in the buildings across the street.

Efforts to develop and implement strategies for linking neighborhood transformation and campus planning set the stage for Penn's long-term growth to the east. Southeast of campus, at the riverfront, we acquired Philadelphia's mothballed former convention-center site. New streets and a grand boulevard are being constructed in addition to new buildings for Penn Medicine and the Children's Hospital of Philadelphia, including the Rafael Viñoly–designed Perelman Center for Advanced Medicine (expected to open in 2008). This work will completely reorganize the urban landscape southeast of the campus and redefine that portion of the Schuylkill riverfront.

In 2004, after years of hard work and even harder political maneuvering and negotiating, Penn acquired the fourteen-acre federal post-office site, a maze of buildings and seven acres of open space due south of the structures at the riverfront. This acquisition will allow the University to link the new eastern end of the Penn campus with Center City, after developing the abandoned buildings that separate Penn from the river.

It is a commonly held view in Philadelphia that, had Penn not been so actively engaged in transforming West Philadelphia, there would have been little political support for, and more likely strong community opposition to, these two major acquisitions of public property. I can attest, firsthand, to how true that is. When I began as president, the medical center had been negotiating with the city for the old convention-center site. The wrangling had been going on for years, with the then president of the City Council, John Street, as the leading opponent. The cost to the University was pegged at $30 million, and several members of City Council, including Mr. Street, thought that rich, powerful Penn would be stealing it at the price. The city was financially strapped, and many looked longingly at Penn's resources. Finally, negotiations broke down, with rancor on both sides. Again, this is all too familiar a tale of the experiences of many inner-city institutions. When John Street, now mayor, signed the deals for the major portions of the property in 2001 and 2003, the city transferred the property to Penn for less than $5 million, and the Commonwealth of Pennsylvania provided a $10 million demolition grant for phase 1 of construction. The full cost for demolition and new building on the entire site will be more than a billion dollars, a portion of it to be expended on local contractors. Estimates suggest that twenty-five hundred construction jobs and seventeen hundred permanent jobs will be created, many for West Philadelphia residents, under the programs described in Chapter 7. Councilwoman Jannie Blackwell glowingly presented these and other economic-impact data when City Council was asked to vote on the acquisition. This was clearly the reflection of a new era for Penn and the city.

Now Penn is also among the leaders of the Schuylkill River Development Corporation (SRDC), a newly created public-private partnership that includes federal, state, and local government, private developers, and civic institutions, which is taking a comprehensive approach to revitalizing the underutilized river corridor through the center of Philadelphia. Over the past ten years, uncoordinated development had been taking place along the Schuylkill riverfront from its confluence with the Delaware River to the Fairmount Dam, a distance of about eight miles. This section of the Schuylkill has been victim to a century of industrialization, losing its lush green banks that once attracted early Dutch explorers. With Penn as part of the committed civic leadership and one of the major stakeholders, the river is now being seen as a unifying presence and economic catalyst for the city of Philadelphia. The coordinated plan is stimulating a holistic strategy for development intended to improve adjacent neighborhoods, create and preserve natural resources, and promote water- and land-based recreation and tourism. Physical improvements to the riverfront are expected to generate more than $2.5 billion in private, public, and institutional investments over the next ten years, producing a dramatic transformation of the waterfront. Penn's new eastern-campus developments represent one critical element.

The guiding principles of the work of SRDC are framed to reknit the fabric of Philadelphia and its communities on both sides of the river to build a stronger, more attractive, and more viable core. (1) Riverfront access and connections, considered a first step to infusing life back into the "hidden river" (the English translation of the Dutch *Schuylkill*), will be improved. A River Park, new pedestrian ramps, bridges, and docks—critical first infrastructure improvements—are already under way. (2) New riverfront destinations, such as space for public gatherings and bicycle paths and parks, will link up with regional and national trail systems. (3) The division between neighborhoods and the river will be reduced by eliminating some of the barriers—railroad tracks and private corporations that restrict public access—that have fenced neighboring communities off from the river. (4) Efforts will focus on improving the physical conditions of the river itself. The tidal Schuylkill River suffers from a proliferation of contaminated former industrial sites, damaged wetlands, and poor water quality. Critical environmental restoration activities—eliminating sources of pollution and restoring natural systems through stormwater management, increasing awareness and stewardship through educational programs, and improving wildlife habitats—will address these conditions.

Finally, SRDC aims to promote and leverage market-driven development. Private development is increasing as a result of the $170 million in public improvements planned for implementation over the next decade. And with a dedicated stakeholder group coordinating development, it is anticipated that public and private investments will be leveraged for maximum impact. For example, in 2001 a group comprised of Penn, Drexel University, the Delaware River Port Authority, the Center City and University City Districts, the city of Philadelphia, the Pennsylvania Department of Community and Economic Development, and the Philadelphia Industrial Development Corporation spearheaded a comprehensive development plan for the area centered around 30th and Market streets (the location of the Beaux Arts Amtrak/Septa train station and the Beaux Arts post office, which Penn has purchased), a strategically located central section of the river. Labeled the Schuylkill Gateway Project, this plan further positioned West Philadelphia as a center for commercial, residential, academic, and medical development while creating a new gateway between Center City and University City. Improvement to the Market Street Bridge and simplification of traffic patterns around 30th Street Station will be major public-works projects dedicated to supporting this new civic vision and collaboration.

Penn is also contributing to the city by leading efforts to accelerate the potential economic impact of the knowledge economy in the region. Educational institutions have been recognized as key resources to knowledge-based urban economic development, and Penn has been driving this agenda for Philadelphia. To lay the groundwork for collaboration, in 2001 we created (and I chaired) the first areawide college and university Presidents Council in collaboration with the Chamber of Commerce. Meeting quarterly, we worked on issues common to the regional educational sector, from PILOTS (payments to the city in lieu of taxes) to shared arts and cultural resources planning and a shared databank for available jobs to facilitate recruitment of two-career couples. Presidents from community colleges, state colleges and universities, large private universities, and small private colleges had not belonged to the same organizations, and many of these presidents had not met until we had our first meeting. But only a year later, this group was seen as a force in the region.

When a report by the Pennsylvania Economy League recognized the importance of greater Philadelphia's "knowledge industry" for driving the region's economic competitiveness, the presidents' group became a natural ally for transforming the findings into action. The study acknowledged that "the greater Philadelphia higher education cluster is, and will continue to be, the region's single greatest asset in the global competition for knowledge-based economic development."[1] It noted that more than eighty colleges and universities and other institutions of higher education are among the area's largest employers. Together, they deliver an economic impact that exceeds $6.4 billion annually. Higher education is also a leading "exporting industry" and brings new dollars into the region through tuition payments, local spending by students and their families, and research funding from the federal government and other entities.

But it is clearly the case that higher education's impact far surpasses the traditional industry contributions of spending, employment, and investment. By virtue of what it produces—educated people and new ideas—a region's knowledge industry of colleges and universities is an asset driving long-term trends, such as population demographics, worker-pool quality, and entrepreneurship. "The Changing Dynamics of Urban America," a 2004 research report prepared for CEOs for Cities, found that the number of residents with a bachelor's degree or above is the single best predictor of per-capita income growth in cities and metropolitan areas.[2]

The Knowledge Industry Partnership (KIP) was formed in 2002 to represent the Greater Philadelphia region and committed itself to three interlocking agendas: attracting talent to the region, creating an educated, skilled worker pool, and stimulating entrepreneurial activity. In the Philadelphia region each school year, an estimated one-quarter of newly enrolled students (almost twenty thousand) come from outside the region, about 1.5 times the rate of foreign immigration to the region. And while area colleges and universities award more than fifty-four thousand degrees annually, only a fraction of these graduates remained in Philadelphia. The city was seen as needing this talent to rejuvenate an aging and shrinking workforce, to raise regional educational attainment levels, and to start entrepreneurial companies that would create new jobs and increase the tax base.

The Knowledge Industry Partnership sought to address these regional advantages and weaknesses in order to maximize the impact of the region's knowledge industry on the economic position of the city. KIP brought together a coalition of civic, business, government, and higher-education partners that was unprecedented for Philadelphia in its breadth of leadership and its cross-representation of interests. KIP is an excellent model of collaboration by a diverse set of partners around a shared agenda.

Unlike some other regional or state initiatives, KIP believed that retaining college students—its ultimate goal—begins with attracting them. And keeping them in the area requires consistent and positive engagement with students throughout their college career, providing them with internships and job opportunities that are viewed as attractive, plentiful, and accessible. To this end, the core strategies driving KIP were organized around the three main phases of the college-student "life cycle": (1) Arrive (the college selection process); (2) Explore (the enrolled student experience); and (3) Achieve (the after-college decision). I served as founding chairperson of KIP's Advisory Group, an overseeing body representing a cross-section of regional organizations and interests. Indicative of KIP's collaborative spirit, three distinguished regional leaders spearhead KIP's working groups, each with a core strategy. The Arrive group, led by Meryl Levitz, president and CEO of the Greater Philadelphia Tourism Maketing Corporation, worked to increase student demand to attend colleges in Greater Philadelphia. The Explore component, under Stephanie Naidoff, commerce director of the City of Philadelphia and city representative, aimed to promote a vibrant college-student experience in the region. The Achieve group, headed by Rich Bendis, president and CEO of Innovation Philadelphia, had as its goal the retention of young, educated people in the area. In order to secure a leadership position for Philadelphia as a regional center for higher education, KIP developed a three-year, multimillion-dollar initiative (launched in April 2003) positioning Philadelphia as "one big campus," a "premier college destination, where the campus is measured in miles not acres," attempting to enrich the academic experience with an exceptional array of off-campus experiences—educational, cultural, professional, and personal.

The Knowledge Industry Partnership represents a shared regional agenda centered on the area's college-student population. But the financial impact of the knowledge economy goes far beyond the multiplier effects of enlarging the pool of talented students. An additional concerted effort was needed that focused on university technology-transfer capacity, and on infrastructure and tax policy to support entrepreneurship and new business development based on research flowing out of university laboratories as well as the innovative start-ups fueled by young entrepreneurs. With world-class research institutions and medical centers, Philadelphia had enormous strength in the life sciences in particular, but its potential to develop, attract, and retain start-ups from all this intellectual capital was minimal at best, with an approach to economic development that focused on individual deals and transactions rather than on long-term strategy and policy. Something very different was needed if Philadelphia was to create an innovation zone that would come close to rivaling Boston/Cambridge, for example.

Leading-edge cities seeking this same brass ring were creating new forms of public-private partnerships. Pittsburgh, Indianapolis, Washington, and Akron were among the growing number of cities that had each launched regional leadership efforts to help change the prevailing economic development mindset in those regions. We all recognized that the success of leading regions like Silicon Valley, Research Triangle, and Austin is based on networks that continually connect people with ideas to others who can develop them into businesses. To emulate this in San Diego, the University of California at San Diego is leading UCConnect, creating robust biotechnology and telecommunications clusters by linking downtown attorneys and service professionals to uptown scientists and engineers. The Greater Phoenix Economic Council and the Kansas Technology Enterprise Corporation are examples of other strong public-private partnerships that have been highly effective.

The challenges were substantial for Philadelphia. Rather than having too few such organizations, it had too many. They were scattered, competitive with one another, and underfunded. Civic leadership was stretched, and, surprisingly, the universities as the engines of innovations were often absent from the table. There were numerous competing planning studies and marketing efforts but no coherent focus on how to harness and increase Philadelphia's real economic potential or capacity.

Penn used some more of the chits it had earned in its neighborhood-development efforts to pull some of these dispersed organizations and competitive factions together, relying on other terrific civic leaders who saw the enormous unrealized potential being squandered. Some organizations merged into the Chamber of Commerce, others relocated to the newly invigorated Science Center, and the CEOs of all relevant organizations and their board chairs began to meet regularly to plan further organizational mergers and integration. It is slow going and still very much a work in progress, but there have been some successes.

To create a more supportive environment, the Commonwealth of Pennsylvania passed enabling legislation to establish Keystone Innovation Zones—physical areas in and around Pennsylvania's education institutions, fostering emergence and growth of new businesses to be fueled by the intellectual capital available in these zones. The program includes tax credits to reward, and create an incentive for, company establishment and growth within the Keystone Innovation

Zones and also tax credits for research and development. It creates a continuum of coordinated services, including access to university research and development labs and facilities, venture capital, "angel" investors, commercial financing, state investment for early stage technology companies, business-development services, and work-force-development benefits. It provides money for Innovation Grants, designed to provide universities and entrepreneurs with the resources to jump-start the transfer of technology through new companies. And with Penn's experience as the role model, the Keystone Innovation Zone program supports the development of a joint economic-growth plan among the educational institutions, economic developers, and the communities around these institutions. In this way, the program stimulates the economic growth and appeal of communities where zones are located, through job creation and training explicitly focused on the residents of those neighborhoods, along with additional ame-nities that improve the quality of life and attractiveness of the com-munity. Customized job training for basic skills and guaranteed free training for advanced skills is expected to be available to Keystone zone residents through workforce-development grants. The goal is to create new "knowledge neighborhoods" that do not leave the poor and unskilled behind.

Many Penn people became deeply engaged in the city and region during this eight-year period of transformation. Penn faculty and senior administrators were encouraged to play a role, and many did. Among us we chaired the Redevelopment Authority, the city Planning Commission, and the Historic Landmarks Board and served on numerous civic and cultural boards. I cochaired John F. Street's mayoral transition team and the several groups described earlier. We were visible, action-oriented participants at a time when corporate consolidation was diminishing the number and capacity of Philadelphia's civic leaders. Again, because of the credibility we had developed through the neighborhood-revitalization work, our participation was welcomed. No longer were we the eight-hundred-pound gorilla, as Penn was disparagingly referred to (a common term applied by many cities to the university in their midst). We were the long-term, committed stakeholder, working to make Philadelphia better. I believe for a university to be truly world class it needs to do great, visible things in its own backyard.

NUMEROUS CHALLENGES REMAIN for the work in West Philadelphia, to be addressed during the coming years. Significant needs still exist in an "outer ring" of blight and instability located outside the original target area. There is the continuing struggle to increase achievement in the local public schools. In some portions of University City and adjacent areas, unemployment and poverty continue to be a problem. In addition, some of the neighborhood commercial corridors are still in need of physical improvement and an even more diverse mix of retailers. While there has been great improvement in the housing market, there is still a relatively low rate of home ownership and a limited supply of quality mixed-income housing in the area. And, despite best efforts, the tension between gentrification and affordability has increased, and the issue needs constant vigilance.

While the revitalization is not yet finished, there have been real and significant improvements in all five areas of intervention: neighborhood safety, capacity, and services have improved, there is a greater number of high-quality diverse housing choices (both homeownership and rental), there has been a significant renewal of retail activity and options, economic development directed toward neighborhood residents and businesses is building more substantial and sustainable capacity, and the public schools are definitely showing improvement. These accomplishments provide a sound base for additional activities in all five areas, which now rely as well on a broader group of investors, developers, and service providers (see box). And Penn is focusing on new ways to attract resources to West Philadelphia. Further money that can be leveraged to develop initiatives—from the private sector, government, and foundations—is crucial, and raising it has been made significantly easier by a record of success.

Penn found that a reorientation of institutional structure, goals, and strategies was essential to the University's effectiveness as both a driving force in the Greater Philadelphia region and as a contributor to the

---

Commitments to University City Leveraging Penn's Investment

In addition to the substantial number of private real estate developers doing work described earlier in Chapters 6 and 9, other significant investors have leveraged investments made by the University of Pennsylvania to University City.

✦ In 2002, Citizens Bank launched a $28 million, five-year University City Neighborhood Improvement Program. The bank's initiative, funded by Citizens in coordination with Penn, included a commitment of $5 million for mortgage loans, $10 million for business loans, $10 million for interim loans to nonprofit and private housing developers, a $15 million acquisition loan pool for nonprofit developers of affordable housing and neighborhood facilities, and a $250,000 fund to provide grants for proposals from University-based nonprofit organizations. Citizens exceeded 300 percent of the bank's overall performance goal within the first eighteen months of this five-year program.

✦ The William Penn Foundation, a Philadelphia-based charitable foundation, named West Philadelphia one of a small number of neighborhoods selected for a targeted grant-making approach to promote more coordinated, strategic investments and policies. Funding has been made available to a number of nonprofit organizations in Penn's University City community, as well as to citywide organizations working in this neighborhood.

✦ West Philadelphia is one of three Philadelphia communities targeted by The Reinvestment Fund (TRF) for investment and other support as part of TRF's Neighborhood Investment Strategy work with the William Penn Foundation. TRF is a financial intermediary that builds wealth and opportunity for low-wealth communities and low- and moderate-income individuals through the promotion of socially and environmentally responsible development. With resources from William Penn that include

economic stability and social well-being of the West Philadelphia community. It was essential for us to reposition the University for a fundamentally different role in the neighborhood, city, and regional economy.

The story told here is clearly not a prescription that can be precisely duplicated by every university. Depending on local realities, such as geography, history, and public- and private-sector conditions, choices must be made about how the roles of leadership/administration and partner-

---

grant support and a $5 million program-related investment, TRF identifies areas of opportunity and then works with partners to move key market-changing projects forward.

＊TRF's rationale for selecting West Philadelphia states: "This area is in rapid transition as the University of Pennsylvania has stepped-up its neighborhood presence and the Penn-supported school continues to attract Penn faculty, graduate students and staff to University City as homeowners and renters. As a result of recent price appreciation, many investment opportunities near the core University City area are being undertaken by private developers. A key part of our strategy for West Philadelphia is to act more proactively to move several critical projects forward that have not yet been undertaken by the market, and to complement these opportunities with preservation activities that improve block appearance and support existing homeowners."

＊The city of Philadelphia's Neighborhood Transformation Initiative (NTI), a new policy launched in 2001 by Mayor John F. Street, provides substantial new resources for neighborhood reinvestment in neighborhoods across the city. A substantial portion of University City has been designated for special consideration as an NTI planning area, and the city has already made significant commitments of NTI funding resources to support West Philadelphia neighborhood-revitalization activities. One recent example is the allocation of NTI funding to acquire vacant properties on Sansom Street, an isolated area of high housing abandonment in an otherwise stable portion of the Spruce Hill neighborhood, to be rehabilitated and sold under a mixed-income housing plan developed by Partnership Community Development Corporation.

Source: John Kromer and Lucy Kerman, *West Philadelphia Initiatives: A Case Study in Urban Revitalization* (Philadelphia: University of Pennsylvania, 2004), pp. 54–55.

---

ship are crafted. In every effort it is crucial, at the outset, to evaluate and invite the most appropriate level and type of participation by government, private, and nonprofit sectors, based on the scope of the initiatives and the determination of which entity has the resources and capacity for effective and timely implementation. But what is core in every case is to replace inaction with action and isolation with partnership. Globalization is affecting the state of cities in the United States and around the world. These changes are creating greater challenges and greater opportunities for urban universities. Their knowledge base, institutional capacity, creativity, and staying power have never been more needed.

A university has the power to be a great agent of change. It has the intellectual, financial, and human resources to take on the challenge of community transformation. It espouses values that embrace shared community, diversity, and engaged discourse. The efforts, however, are unlikely to reach these ambitious goals quickly or easily—as I tried to show in the preceding chapters. Partly this is due to the complexity and risk of the work, and partly it is due to difficulties of authentic participation—converting skeptical bystanders into engaged stakeholders. Penn had to overcome decades of hostile relations with its neighbors to succeed. We had to encourage critical faculty members to understand and support deployment of fungible resources on nonacademic (in their most literal sense) expenditures. We had to embrace local officials as partners. It was challenging work that required continuous and deep engagement. But with honest self-assessment, strategic planning, reliance on sound urban theory, measurable implementation goals, and some good luck, Penn and its partners did help to transform the neighborhood. By reorienting the way we worked, with whom we worked, and what we were willing to commit, we found a way to help make the neighborhood prosper. Sure, many residents who used to rail against Penn are still screaming at us. But now that they are at the table, they do not shout quite as much or quite as loudly.

A decade ago, the neighborhood could not register even a blip on any private developer's radar screen. Now public-private partnerships are blossoming, and the West Philadelphia Initiatives are winning national and international awards and competitions for design, creative land use, and economic impact, including the prestigious Urban Land Institute's 2003 Award for Excellence. Many of Penn's senior leaders have been honored repeatedly by a variety of civic, governmental, and professional organizations for their role in these efforts.

Today Penn celebrates its ongoing transformation into a world-class urban research university that is nourished by the neighborhood it helped to develop and revitalize. Far from robbing Penn's academic future to pay for this progress, the University's engagement as urban developer has played a critical role in enhancing Penn's academic reputation. All the markers of academic success—rankings, faculty awards, student applications, selectivity, growth in endowment—have soared to record levels. Our *U.S. News and World Report* ranking (the measure all university presidents love to hate) went from sixteenth to fourth during my ten years as president. These and more valid measures produced by professional associations and the National Academies are important to cite, not as a boast, but because, no matter how well endowed an institution, there never seems to be enough money for all the excellent academic and cocurricular programs. Yet our investment in West Philadelphia paid strong academic dividends as well and could be an example for colleges and universities trying to win over their own skeptical stakeholders to similar undertakings.

From our experience in West Philadelphia, we learned several valuable lessons about strategies and practices that can transform urban neighborhoods and help cities become great places in which to live and work.

First, any successful urban strategy must be just that—strategic. It must be bold yet based on a realistic and full assessment of social, economic, and political forces at work, and it must have a clear roadmap toward implementation. Today, neighborhood-change efforts in cities occur amid four decades of deindustrialization, two generations of suburbanization, and the emergence of "edge cities." While the revival of some big city downtowns indicates a renewed appreciation for urban amenities, most urban neighborhoods in older U.S. cities are still poor and heavily populated with minorities. A good strategic framework identifies and articulates potential obstacles for such complex work and is a critical first step toward success.

An overall strategy includes planning for resource deployment. To give an example, we created a 2x2 matrix to evaluate capacity for real-estate development, our largest and most visible set of expenditures (Figure 12). One dimension assessed market readiness and the other Penn's financial capacity or willingness. Where market readiness was seen as anti-investment, the University had to assess its own financial resources and tolerance for risk, since many of these projects required significant subsidies and weak or no financial-return ratios on investment. Where market readiness for investment was more positive, the University sought to protect its investments and share in potential upside. At the start of the West Philadelphia Initiatives, Penn's strategy was to

Figure 12
Real Estate
Development
Strategy Matrix.
Numbers in
circles equal
overall cost of
project, including
non-Penn
investors.

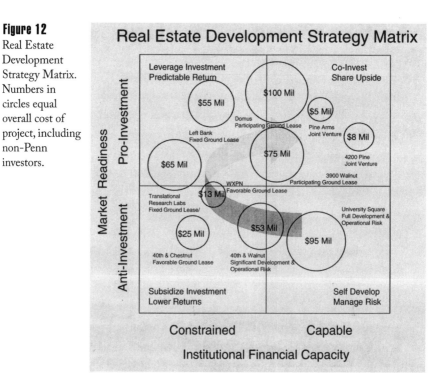

create or incubate the real-estate market, which was largely inactive, as the sole investor. The lower left and right quadrants of Figure 12 describe the key investments made with University funds when market forces were not motivating private-sector investment and the University was willing to take on full risk in order to stimulate market forces. As the market developed, the strategy was to stimulate and engage the market as coinvestor (upper left quadrant). The final phase of the strategy envisioned other investors as market leaders (upper right quadrant), where the university could share in the upside. The Appendix describes the design of each investment more fully.

Second, we have seen that a holistic approach has a greater chance of both capitalizing on resources more effectively and promoting greater sustainability. Figure 13 shows the overlap of initiatives in the five domains of intervention. The positive effect of multiple active efforts under way cannot be underestimated, and some concurrent intervention on several fronts signals commitment and creates leverage. Retail amenities that generate pedestrian traffic also discourage crime. But business owners will not locate their stores or restaurants in a neighborhood where bold measures are not already being taken to reduce crime and eliminate blight. Likewise, incentives such as employee-assistance mortgage programs that promote home ownership are vital. It is a win-win situation when urban-based businesses and institutions make a greater effort to encourage their employees to live close by. Cutting down on long commutes is good for the environment, for mental health, and for the community. But unless there are excellent public-school options, middle-class families will stay away and put up with longer commutes. Economic development, public education, home ownership, and safe neighborhoods are all essential pieces of a healthy community.

Third, collaboration and transparency are critical to success. As a psychologist, I wrestled with these issues of trust and participation. My own research on choice and control had demonstrated that significant positive outcomes result from individuals' perceptions that they have a say in decisions, and that they have relevant and important options from which to choose.[1] What I tried to do was to put some of these findings into action.

Figure 13

Geographic Overlap of West Philadelphia Initiatives as of June 2, 2004. Numbers
correspond to Initatives goals: (1) Improve neighborhood safety, services, and
capacities. (2) Provide high-quality, diverse housing choices. (3) Revive commercial
activity. (4) Accelerate economic development. (5) Enhance local public school
options. John Kromer and Lucy Kerman, *West Philadelphia Initiatives: A Case Study
in Urban Revitalization* (Philadelphia: University of Pennsylvania, 2004), p. 53.

I knew it was important for people to participate and work toward shared
goals, and that their doing so produced better results. And being mindful
of giving credit to others, often and generously, is crucial. By increasing
the neighbors' sense of control and empowering them to have a voice and
real options for action, we increased chances for meaningfully changing
behavior and improving social outcomes. Yet initially these efforts were
often challenged and met with suspicion. This is not surprising, since most
large institutions do not give their neighbors many reasons to believe that
ordinary people can shape public outcomes in meaningful ways. Opening

decision-making processes, inviting civic engagement, and learning from input on the ground are essential components for success in this type of community-development work. Most inner-city neighborhood residents around universities recognize that they face complex problems requiring collaborative solutions, yet they feel that collaboration is unwelcome. We had to confront these attitudes and show what was different, time and time again.

To truly become a citizen of the community and a more trusted agent of change, Penn had to reconstruct the very nature of its relationship to the neighborhood into one that ran through everything we represented as an institution—from our research to our teaching, from student volunteerism to real-estate and economic development. We networked with every community development corporation, every block association and community group, every political and social activist, and every internal constituency. It was messy and time consuming, but the effort worked.

There is an important distinction between developing common aims and seeking consensus. While we worked hard to engage our neighbors as partners, to enhance their opportunity for deliberative input, this is not the same as seeking consensus. Consensus-seeking is a process that often results in vague goals and least-common-denominator actions with weak impact. Common purpose better reconciles competing values.[2]

Fourth, we learned that an institution that appears rich to others must be extremely careful about raising expectations. There is risk in developing an open deliberative process, diagnosing needs, and seeking allies when the balance of access to resources—real and perceived—is so one-sided. Setting clear expectations, being willing to say what we could not, or would not, do, was critical. But identifying and acting on a few major initiatives was crucial in earning the ability to decline requests as well. We provided access to sound, objective data for decision-making whenever possible because emotions often ran high around the issues being addressed. Facts enable more full and real deliberations, and make the basis for choices clearer. That is not to say that we were always the most conservative voice in the room. A university should be about agitating for change, about advocating new and sometimes very controversial solutions to long-standing problems. That was often the position in which we found ourselves.

Fifth, while time is short, patience must always be long. Setbacks, delays, and criticism are inevitable, and Penn experienced its share of all these things. We certainly did not anticipate the movie-theater debacle, and for a time it stopped us in our tracks. And in the same vein, for a period the development of the Penn-assisted public school divided the community and brought the wrath of some upon the University. But in both these cases, the University stayed the course with regard to its overall strategy while modifying specific plans as appropriate. Being able to learn from mistakes and to make modifications accordingly is critical.

No agenda for change, however well conceived, well received, or successfully implemented, wins unanimous raves. But when alliances are formed with relevant stakeholders, more and more allies can be recruited. We learned that a university can play a lead role in urban transformation by changing its perspective and making a commitment to alter its ways of interacting and transacting. Penn was already spending tens of millions of dollars a year on construction and purchasing every year. By reorienting itself toward fostering relationships with local businesses, the University found a way for them to prosper together with us. By inviting our neighbors to join us at the table as partners in the shared work of beautifying the streets and parks, improving the public schools, reviving the commercial corridors, and reanimating the housing market, we found a way to live more productively together.

If you are fortunate in life, you will be given the opportunity to do work you love in a place you love. I had the great privilege of leading the University of Pennsylvania, my alma mater, in the city where my parents spent their lives and where I was raised. And each time I return to University City, as I often do, it is a thrill to experience its vibrancy and to know that I had a part in the transformation. As I said about that baseball team of neighborhood kids I was lucky enough to have on the street where I grew up, it does not get any better than that.

Projects Developed Under West Philadelphia Initiatives

The major real estate projects developed under the West Philadelphia Initiatives are Translational Research Laboratory (TRL), WXPN/ World Café Live, The Left Bank, Domus Apartments (3401 Chestnut Street), University Square, 3900 Walnut Street, Upper 40th Street (two projects, Metropolitan and Teres), 40th and Walnut Streets, Pine Arms (305–311 S. 40th Street), and 4200 Pine Street. The projects are discussed in order of geographic location, from east to west.

Translational Research Laboratory (TRL)

125 South 31st Street

TOTAL DEVELOPMENT COST: $75 million

SCHOOL OF MEDICINE FIT-OUT: $35 million

TOTAL SQUARE FOOTAGE: 130,000 gross square feet

OCCUPANCY: October 2004

DEVELOPER: Forest City Commercial Group

ARCHITECTS: Tsoi Kobus – Base Building; Nalls Architecture – School of Medicine

REAL ESTATE STRUCTURE: A ground lease was granted to Forest City, with a leaseback to University of Pennsylvania School of Medicine. The ground lease term is sixty-five years. The School of Medicine lease has an initial term of twenty years with two twenty-year and one five-year renewals. This lease is triple net with an annual rent of $4.6 million during the first five years, increasing in increments to $6.1 million in the last five years of the initial term.

UNIVERSITY STRATEGY: Leverage Investment. TRL was developed to fulfill the School of Medicine's need for wet bench biomedical research laboratory space, mammalian and nonmammalian animal holding and testing space, and spin-off translational research uses by affiliated or third-party users. Internal fit-out was completed in two phases. The School of Medicine subsequently required the entire building for their research needs. Other tenants include radiation safety (ULAR), Center for Neurobiology and Behavior, Center for Sleep, Pulmonary, and Emergency Medicine. The ground lease payments back to the University were fixed.

WXPN/World Café Live

3025 Walnut Street

TOTAL DEVELOPMENT COST: $13 million

WXPN FIT-OUT: $3.2 million

TOTAL SQUARE FOOTAGE: 43,000 gross square feet

WXPN SQUARE FOOTAGE: 13,000 gross square feet

OCCUPANCY: October 2004

DEVELOPER: Dranoff Properties

ARCHITECTS: Bower Lewis Thrower – Base Building; Meyer
   Associates – WXPN; DAS – World Café Live

REAL ESTATE STRUCTURE: A fifty-year ground lease was granted to Dranoff Properties, with a fifteen-year leaseback to WXPN with two five-year renewals. The WXPN lease is triple net and has a net present value (NPV) of $4.5 million, based on a 6 per cent discount rate. The developer secured historic tax credits, and the economic benefit will be split among partners, in proportion to the economic effect. The building, constructed in 1921 with an Art Deco facade for the Hajoca Corporation, is eligible for designation on the National Register of Historic Places and is a contributory building to the West Philadelphia historic district.

UNIVERSITY STRATEGY: Subsidize investment. WXPN, Penn's commercial-free radio station, was housed in two separate locations: its broadcast studios in an antiquated residential structure, and its offices in a commercial office building. WXPN/World Café Live was developed to bring the radio station's units together, provide visually compelling street-level broadcast studios for the University's public radio station and a live performance venue/restaurant linked to the station's nationally syndicated radio program *World Café*. A private investor provided funding for the World Café Live fit out and operation; WXPN supported the station fit out from its endowment. The building had been vacant for a number of years and the strategy was intended to animate the streetscape at the eastern edge of campus. The ground lease payments back to the University were fixed.

The Left Bank

3131 Walnut Street

TOTAL DEVELOPMENT COST: $70 million

TOTAL UNIT COUNT: 282 units of luxury apartments. A former General Electric warehouse on the eastern edge of Penn's campus which stretches over an entire city block has been renovated into The Left Bank, a mixed-use building which includes 282 luxury apartment units, 14,000 square-feet of street-fronted retail space, high-tech offices housing hundreds of Penn employees, the Penn's Children Center (childcare center), and an indoor parking facility. More than 235 residential parking spaces are located within the structure at the first and second floors.

OCCUPANCY: January 2001

DEVELOPER: Dranoff Properties of Philadelphia

ARCHITECT: Bower Lewis and Thrower

REAL ESTATE STRUCTURE: The University purchased the property in 1996 and remains its owner, but entered into a long-term lease with Dranoff Properties for the $70 million conversion. Ground lease payments were fixed in advance. The developer secured historic tax credits, and the economic benefit will be split among partners, in proportion to the economic effect. The building was eligible for designation on the National Register of Historic Places and is a contributory building to the West Philadelphia historic district.

UNIVERSITY STRATEGY: Leverage investment. The Facilities and Real Estate Department of the University of Pennsylvania was housed together for the first time, creating synergies and economies of scale. They are located on the ground floor of the Left Bank, in office space that received several architectural awards. A Penn child care center, fulfilling significant needs for Penn affiliates, was built at the street level of the Left Bank apartments. Retail space also animates the streetscape.

Opened in 2001, the apartments fill a void in the luxury housing market of University City by providing valuable living space to professionals and others associated with the academic, technology and medical institutions just blocks away who want to live close to work. Further, its proximity to Philadelphia's 30th Street Station, Route I-76, and I-95 provides access to the entire region.

Domus Apartments

3401 Chestnut Street

TOTAL DEVELOPMENT COST: $100 million

TOTAL UNIT COUNT: 290 luxury apartments (total 340,000 gross square feet), averaging 1,100 square feet each, with amenities of 320-space, six-story parking garage, heated outdoor pool, 24/7 fitness facility, multimedia business conference center; 21,000 gross square feet of ground-floor retail along Chestnut and 34th.

EXPECTED OCCUPANCY: Fall 2007

DEVELOPER: Hanover Company

ARCHITECT: Design Collective, Inc.

REAL ESTATE STRUCTURE: A sixty-five-year ground lease was granted to Hanover/MetLife partnership. Participating ground lease payments will be paid relative to cash flows with a guaranteed amount.

UNIVERSITY STRATEGY: Leverage investment. Conversion of 2.6-acre parking lot into luxury apartments and retail. This property was formerly owned by the Redevelopment Authority of Philadelphia. The terms of sale to the University required redevelopment of site as residential, with supporting retail, office, and parking. The campus development plan calls for mixed-use residential development adjacent to Hill Field at 34th and Chestnut streets, across from this property.

University Square

3600 Block of Walnut Street

TOTAL DEVELOPMENT COST: $95 million

TOTAL SQUARE FOOTAGE: 300,000 square feet, including 12 retail shops and 290 first-class hotel rooms

OCCUPANCY: 1999–2000

DEVELOPER: University of Pennsylvania

ARCHITECT: Elkus Manfredi

REAL ESTATE STRUCTURE: Overall financing for the development came through an internal funding mechanism of The University of Pennsylvania through which Penn contributed 100 percent of the development costs. The University expected a 7 percent return on equity. Within the first three years of operation the project covered most of its debt service burden.

UNIVERSITY STRATEGY: Self-develop. Given the lack of interest by the real estate market, the University had no choice but to take the full role of a developer managing the risks of development and operations. The project was created to change the landscape at the core of the campus and provide a hub of retail and hospitality. As described in Chapter 7, this project houses the Inn at Penn, managed by Hilton Hotels, the Penn Bookstore, and numerous restaurants and shops to stimulate foot traffic and animate the streets.

3900 Walnut

TOTAL DEVELOPMENT COST: $75 million

TOTAL UNIT COUNT: 450 beds market-rate student housing. 50,000 gross square footage of ground-floor retail along Walnut Street.

OCCUPANCY: Fall 2009

DEVELOPER: First Worthing University Partners

ARCHITECT: Erdy McHenry, Philadelphia.

REAL ESTATE STRUCTURE: A sixty-five-year ground lease was granted to First Worthing. Participating ground lease payments relative to cash flows with a guaranteed amount.

UNIVERSITY STRATEGY: Leverage investment. Conversion of approximately two-acre site with one-story strip mall built in the 1970s into a mixed-use student apartments and retail. The campus development plan called for mixed-use residential development. Provisions were made for subsidized artist live and work space as well as a diverse retail mix.

40th and Walnut Streets

TOTAL DEVELOPMENT COST: $53 million

TOTAL SQUARE FOOTAGE: three facilities—35,000 square foot grocery store (Fresh Grocer) with 700 parking spaces; 40,000 square foot, six-screen cinema and lounge (the Bridge); 7,595 square foot restaurant and entertainment venue (Marathon Grill)

OCCUPANCY: May 2001 (Fresh Grocer); November 2002 (the Bridge); Summer 2004 (Marathon Grill)

DEVELOPER: University of Pennsylvania

ARCHITECT: Wood and Zapata, spg3, Powerstrip (cinema interior)

REAL ESTATE STRUCTURE: Overall financing for the development came through an internal funding mechanism of The University of Pennsylvania through which Penn contributed 100% of the development costs. The University originally expected a 7–8 percent return on equity; however the first years of the development are seeing a return on equity closer to 5 percent. This is a result of the increased costs of developing the cinema for the University by approximately $13 million upon the bankruptcy of the original partner. This development is now one of the most successful retail destinations in the City of Philadelphia with the Fresh Grocer gross sales topping $800 per square foot and the cinema ranking consistently among the top-grossing in the region.

UNIVERSITY STRATEGY: Self-develop. The University purchased the western lots for redevelopment of anchor locations as part of the West Philadelphia Initiative, and its success today confirms the University's initial conviction that retail development could improve the quality of that intersection by providing retail amenities servicing both residents and students, while supporting neighborhood commerce.

Upper 40th Street

Metropolis Group

TOTAL DEVELOPMENT COST: $1.7 million

TOTAL SQUARE FOOTAGE: 11 rowhouse buildings on 40th Street, Ludlow Street, and Chestnut Street, totaling 3,000 square feet retail and 17 residential units

OCCUPANCY: Fall 2006

DEVELOPER: Metropolis Group

ARCHITECT: Cicada Architecture Planning

REAL ESTATE STRUCTURE: Since the university was unwilling to commit the capital resources to undertake the required redevelopment, yet was convinced the buildings were strategically located, the properties were ground leased to the Metropolis Group for fifty years. Metropolis will pay a flat original rent with escalations. Metropolis raised the capital, supervised the redevelopment, and will own and operate the improvements until the end of the lease. At the end of the lease the University will repossess the properties. This redevelopment is already repopulating 40th Street and will increase retail offerings while increasing 40th Street's appeal as a destination.

UNIVERSITY STRATEGY: Subsidize investment. These properties were bought by the University of Pennsylvania to reverse the trend of physical decline in the adjacent neighborhood. Because 40th Street is where campus meets community, and retail is a critical component of community development, further development of properties in this area is a crucial element of the University's strategy.

Upper 40th Street

Teres Holdings

3943–45 Chestnut Street

104 S. 40th Street

4001 Chestnut Street

TOTAL DEVELOPMENT COST: $23.5 million

TOTAL SQUARE FOOTAGE: 3 buildings, 28,000 square feet of retail, 103 units, 157 beds

OCCUPANCY: Summer 2006

DEVELOPER: Teres Holdings

ARCHITECT: Piatt Associates

REAL ESTATE STRUCTURE: Fifty-year ground lease structure to Teres Holdings for fifty years with two renewal options. Teres Holdings pays a flat fee plus a percentage participatory rent. Teres Holdings raised the capital, supervised the redevelopment and will own and operate the improvements until the end of the lease. At the expiration of the options the University will repossess the properties.

UNIVERSITY STRATEGY: Subsidize investment. Since the university did not have the capital resources to commit to the required redevelopment yet was convinced the buildings were strategically located, the properties were ground leased. These properties were bought by the University of Pennsylvania in reaction to the accelerated decline of physical assets close to its campus. Many of the buildings in this package were vacant and needing a major infusion of capital. Given that the community also considered these buildings part of their resources, the University undertook a process of consultation with community groups and helped form the Friends of 40th Street. The consultations resulted in the establishment of development guidelines and have helped to improve relationships between the university and the community.

The retail mix in the newly created 28,000 square feet of retail has further contributed to making 40th Street a destination. The amenities program includes: landscaped pedestrian promenade, traffic calming architectural elements, store-fronts and retail businesses with strong curb appeal, public art, apartments overlooking terraces, street performance space and seating, "Café Alley" outdoor food service, kiosks and artist vending.

Pine Arms

305–311 S. 40th Street

TOTAL DEVELOPMENT COST: $4.97 million

UNIT COUNT: 41 one- and two-bedroom apartments

OCCUPANCY: Spring 2003

DEVELOPER: Campus Apartments

REAL ESTATE STRUCTURE: The transaction, completed in October 2002, assured the complete rehabilitation of the property. The property consists of 41 one- and two-bedroom apartments. The transaction was structured so that the approximately $3.8 million rehabilitation project would be completed with no cash outlay by Penn. The transaction is classified as a nonmonetary exchange of property to a limited partnership in which the University will own a 50 percent interest as limited partner.

A local property manager and developer, Campus Apartments, acting as general partner on behalf of the partnership, obtained, guaranteed, and secured bank loan financing in order to renovate the property. The developer supervised the improvements and manages the property under the terms of a Construction Management and Property Management agreement on behalf of the partnership. The value of the University's contribution to the partnership is stipulated to be $900,000. The University recovered an additional $100,000 from the general partner. The total project costs, including other partner's equity and loans and acquisition, were approximately $4.97 million.

The developer was expected to secure historic tax credits, and the economic benefit was split among partners, in proportion to the economic effect. The building is eligible for designation on the national register of historic places and is a contributory building to the West Philadelphia historic district.

UNIVERSITY STRATEGY: Co-invest—share upside. Penn needed to reposition student residential assets in disrepair in a key location to attract graduate and professional students back to University City from Center City. It was expected that demand would grow as the neighborhood improved.

4200 Pine Street

TOTAL DEVELOPMENT COST: $7.8 million

TOTAL SQUARE FOOTAGE: 27 residential condominiums
   plus a 9,750 square-feet mansion designed by
   Horace T. Trumbauer

OCCUPANCY: Winter 2006–2007

DEVELOPER: Campus Apartments

ARCHITECT: Qb3

REAL ESTATE STRUCTURE: Redeveloped in partnership with an independent developer, the University contributed the land and building to the partnership while the developer provided the capital, supervised construction and sold the units. The University will retain a percentage of the proceeds.

UNIVERSITY STRATEGY: Co-invest—share upside. This building complex, located in the middle of a residential community, originally housed four university administrative departments. The departments were relocated to campus, and the offices were converted into luxury condominiums. This redevelopment is expected to create new home ownership opportunities within the Penn Alexander School area and become an attractive alternative in the condominium market of Philadelphia.

CHAPTER 1. MOBILIZING FOR ACTION

1. Jane Jacobs, *The Death and Life of Great American Cities* (New York: Random House, 1961).

2. Ibid.

3. David Brooks, "The Education Gap," *New York Times,* September 25, 2005.

CHAPTER 2. WHY NEIGHBORHOOD REVITALIZATION

1. John O. Norquist, *The Wealth of Cities: Revitalizing the Centers of American Life* (Reading, Mass.: Addison-Wesley, 1998).

2. Ira Harkavy and Harmon Zuckerman, *Eds and Meds: Cities' Hidden Assets,* in Survey Series: Center on Urban and Metropolitan Policy (Washington, D.C.: Brookings Institution, 1999).

3. Ibid.

4. Initiative for a Competitive Inner City and CEOS for Cities, *Leveraging Colleges and Universities for Urban Economic Revitalization: An Action Agenda,* 2002.

5. Richard L. Palm and J. Douglas Toma, "Community Relationships and Partnerships," *New Directions for Student Services,* 1997, no. 79, pp. 57–65.

6. Initiative for a Competitive Inner City and CEOS for Cities, *Leveraging Colleges and Universities for Urban Economic Revitalization.*

7. David C. Perry and Wim Wiewel (eds.), *The University as Urban Developer: Case Studies and Analysis,* Cities and Contemporary Society series (Cambridge, Mass.: Lincoln Institute of Land Policy, 2005).

8. Ibid.

9. Paul Fain, "Penn Seen as a Model for Community Partnerships," *Chronicle of Higher Education,* July 22, 2005; R. M. Freeland, "Universities and Cities Need to Rethink Their Relationships," *Chronicle of Higher Education,* May 13, 2005; "Where We Live—Report on Life in University City," *Philadelphia Inquirer,* September 22, 2004, section City—D; Lois Romano, "Urban Colleges Learn to Be Good Neighbors: Universities also Reap Benefits from Investing in Their Communities," *Washington Post,* January 9, 2000, A1.

10. Wilfried Ward, *Life of John Henry Cardinal Newman: Based on His Private Journals and Correspondence, In Two Volumes* (New York: Longmans, Green, 1912), chapter 13.

11. Ahmed M. Kathrada and Robert Vassen, *Letters from Robben Island: A Selection of Ahmed Kathrada's Prison Correspondence, 1964–1989* (East Lansing: Michigan State University Press, 1999), p. 39.

12. Thomas Ehrlich, "Civic Engagement," in *Measuring Up 2000: The State-by-State Report Card for Higher Education* (San Jose, Calif.: National Center for Public Policy and Higher Education, 2000).

13. Roberta B. Gratz and Norman Mintz, *Cities Back from the Edge: New Life for Downtown* (New York: Preservation Press, 1998).

14. David Boehlke, "Great Neighborhoods, Great City," paper prepared for the Goldseker Foundation, 2004.

15. Elise M. Bright, *Reviving America's Forgotten Neighborhoods: An Investigation of Inner-City Revitalization Efforts* (New York: Garland, 2000).

16. Ross J. Gittell and Avis Vidal, *Community Organizing: Building Social Capital as a Development Strategy* (Thousand Oaks, Calif.: Sage Publications, 1998).

17. David P. Varady and Jeffrey A. Raffel, *Selling Cities: Attracting Homebuyers Through Schools and Housing Programs* (Thousand Oaks, Calif.: Sage Publications, 1995).

18. Michael R. Greenberg, "Improving Neighborhood Quality: A Hierarchy of Needs," *Housing Policy Debate* 10, no. 3 (1999): 601–24.

CHAPTER 3. THE GROWTH OF UNIVERSITY CITY

1. Steven M. Friedman, "A Brief History of The University of Pennsylvania," 1996, University Archives and Records Center, University of Pennsylvania, http://archives. unpenn.edu/histy/genlhistory/brief.html.

2. http://www.infoplease.com/ipea/A0154485.html.

3. Carolyn Adams, David Bartelt, David Elesh, Ira Goldstein, Nancy Kleniewski, and William Yancey, *Philadelphia: Neighborhoods, Divisions, and Conflict in a Postindustrial City* (Philadelphia: Temple University Press, 1991).

4. Richard A. Farnum, Jr., "The Road Not Taken," *Pennsylvania Gazette*, November 1996, pp. 17–21.

5. Margaret P. O'Mara, "Learning from History: How State and Local Public Policy Choices Have Shaped Philadelphia's Growth," *Greater Philadelphia Regional Review*, Spring 2002, p. 16.

6. Scott Cohen, "Urban Renewal in West Philadelphia: An Examination of Penn's Planning Expansion and Community Role from the Mid-1940s to the Mid-1970s," senior thesis, University of Pennsylvania, Philadelphia, April 6, 1998, p. 38.

7. Ibid., p. 28.

8. *Philadelphia Inquirer*, March 19, 1960.

9. Quoted in Mackenzie S. Carlson, "Come to Where the Knowledge Is: A History of the University City Science Center," University Archives and Records Center, University of Pennsylvania, September 1999, part 3.

10. James M. O'Neill and Karen Q. Miller, "The Power of Penn," *Inquirer Magazine*, September 19, 1999.

11. Adams et al., *Philadelphia,* p. 17.

12. *Priorities for Neighborhood Revitalization (PFSNI): Goals for the Year 2000,* October 1993, http://www.upenn.edu/almanac/issues/past/PFSNI.html.

13. *The Spruce Hill Community Renewal Plan,* 1995, http://sprucehilca.org/development/plan.html.

14. Jane Brooks, interview with Stephen Schutt, March 9, 2004.

CHAPTER 4. POLICY, ORGANIZATION, AND PLANNING

1. Lewis D. Hopkins, *Urban Redevelopment: The Logic of Making Plans* (Washington, D.C.: Island Press, 2001).

2. Jane Brooks, interview with Pat Clancy, April 1, 2004.

3. Jane Brooks, interview with Gilbert Casellas, November 22, 2004.

4. Jane Brooks, interview with Carol Scheman, March 25, 2004.

5. Charles E. Lindblom, *Inquiry and Change: The Troubled Attempt to Understand and Shape Society* (New Haven: Yale University Press, 1990).

6. James C. Scott, *Seeing Like a State: How Certain Schemes to Improve the Human Condition Have Failed* (New Haven: Yale University Press, 1998).

7. Peter Medoff and Holly Sklar, *Streets of Hope: The Fall and Rise of an Urban Neighborhood* (Boston: South End Press, 1994).

8. Douglas C. Henton, John Melville, and Kimberly Walesh, *Civic Revolutionaries: Igniting the Passion for Change in America's Communities* (San Francisco: Jossey-Bass, 2004).

CHAPTER 5. MAKING THE NEIGHBORHOOD CLEAN AND SAFE

1. Jane Jacobs, *The Death and Life of Great American Cities* (New York: Random House, 1961).

2. James Q. Wilson and George L. Kelling, "Broken Windows," *Atlantic Monthly,* March 1982, p. 31.

3. Malcolm Gladwell, *The Tipping Point: How Little Things Can Make a Big Difference* (Boston: Little, Brown, 2000), p. 142.

4. Jane Brooks, interview with Barry Grossbach, March 25, 2004.

5. Gladwell, *Tipping Point,* p. 167.

6. Robert D. Putnam, *Bowling Alone: The Collapse and Revival of American Community* (New York: Simon & Schuster, 2000).

7. Jacobs, *Death and Life of Great American Cities,* p. 128.

8. *University City Report Card* (Philadelphia: University City District, 2004).

9. Jane Brooks, interview with John Fry, May 28, 2004.

10. Ibid.

CHAPTER 6. RECLAIMING HOUSING

1. Lucy Kerman and John Kromer, *West Philadelphia Initiatives: A Case Study in Urban Revitalization* (Philadelphia: University of Pennsylvania, 2004), p. 26.

2. Richard P. Taub, D. Garth Taylor, and Jan D. Dunham, *Paths of Neighborhood Change: Race and Crime in Urban America* (Chicago: University of Chicago Press, 1984).

3. Rolf Goetze, *Understanding Neighborhood Change: The Role of Expectations in Urban Revitalization* (Cambridge, Mass.: Ballinger, 1979).

4. Jane Brooks, interview with Kate Ward Gaus, December 20, 2004.

5. Kerman and Kromer, *West Philadelphia Initiatives*, p. 31.

6. Maureen Kennedy and Paul Leonard, *Dealing with Neighborhood Change: A Primer on Gentrification and Policy Choices* (Washington, D.C.: Brookings Institution, 2001).

7. Michael E. Porter, "The Competitive Advantage of the Inner City," *Harvard Business Review* (May–June 1995), pp. 55–71.

CHAPTER 7. INVIGORATING THE LOCAL ECONOMY

1. Rolf Goetze, *Understanding Neighborhood Change: The Role of Expectations in Urban Revitalization* (Cambridge, Mass.: Ballinger, 1979), p. 8.

2. Roger S. Ahlbrandt and Paul C. Brophy, *Neighborhood Revitalization: Theory and Practice* (Lexington, Mass.: Heath, 1975).

3. Jane Brooks, interview with Omar Blaik, March 30, 2004.

4. "Design Guidelines and Review of Campus Projects," *Almanac*, 49, no. 6, October 1, 2002, pp. 1–11.

5. Andres Duany, "The New Urbanism and the Center Cities," paper presented at the Twenty-first Century Neighborhoods Conference, October 8, 1998, Philadelphia.

6. Richard Florida, *The Rise of the Creative Class: And How It's Transforming Work, Leisure, Community, and Everyday Life* (New York: Basic Books, 2002).

CHAPTER 8. INVESTING IN PUBLIC EDUCATION

1. Jane Jacobs, *The Death and Life of Great American Cities* (New York: Random House, 1961), p. 113.

2. "Schools in a Cluster: Hornbeck's Idea Seems to be a Good One, But There are Big Questions Remaining," *Philadelphia Inquirer* editorial, November 26, 1994.

3. Dale Mezzacappa, "School Reform Tab: $300 Million; Phila. District a Shambles, Study Says," *Philadelphia Inquirer,* September 16, 1994.

4. "The Annenberg Challenge: Overview," www.annenberginstitute.org/challenge/about/about.htm.

5. Kathleen Cushman, "Community and Critical Friendships: School Change as Everybody's Work," *Journal of the Annenberg Challenge* 1, no. 1 (1997), p. 6.

6. Department of Education Web site, Senate Bill No. 123, passed June 12, 1997, http://www.kiponline.org/homef.htm.

7. Partners for Excellence, "Coalition for Community Schools" (Washington, D.C.: Coalition for Community Schools, 2002).

8. Jane Brooks, interview with Kate Ward Gaus, December 20, 2004.

9. Penn Faculty and Staff for Neighborhood Issues, "Priorities for Neighborhood Revitalization: Goals for the Year 2000," *Almanac*, 40, no. 9 (October 26, 1993), p. 6; Sandy Smith, "Penn–Spruce Hill Effort Wins Award," *Almanac*, 43, no. 19 (January 28, 1997), p. 11.

10. Philadelphia Inquirer, *Report Card on the Schools 2004*, http://inquirer.philly.com/specials/2004/report_card.

11. Lisa Heschong, "Windows and Classrooms: A Study of Student Performance and the Indoor Environment," http://www.energy.ca.gov/reports/2003-11-17_500-03-082_A-07.PDF (California Energy Commission, Public Interest Energy Research [PIER] Program, Sacramento, October 2003). L. Heschong, "Daylighting in Schools: An Investigation into the Relationship Between Daylighting and Human Performance," http://www.pge.com/003_save_energy/ (submitted by the Heschong Mahone Group to Pacific Gas and Electric, on behalf of the California Board for Energy Efficiency Third Party Program, 1999).

12. Jeremy D. Finn, DeWayne Fulton, Jayne Zaharias, and Barbara A. Nye, "Carry-over Effects of Small Classes," *Peabody Journal of Education* 67, no. 1 (1989–1992): 75, 84. Jeremy D. Finn, S. B. Gerber, C. M. Achilles, and J. Boyd-Zaharias, "The Enduring Effects of Small Classes," *Teachers College Record* 103 (2001): 145–83. E. Word, J. Johnston, H. Bain, D. B. Fulton, J. Boyd-Zaharias, M. N. Lintz, C. M. Achilles, J. Folger, and C. Breda, *Student/Teacher Achievement Ratio (STAR): Tennessee's K 3 Class-size Study* (Nashville: Tennessee State Department of Education, 1990).

13. Philadelphia Inquirer, *Report Card on the Schools, 2004*.

14. Robert Wood Johnson Foundation, *Healthy Schools for Healthy Kids*, special report (Princeton, N.J.: Pyramid Communications, 2004), pp. 39–41.

CHAPTER 9. CIVIC LEADERSHIP

1. Pennsylvania Economy League, *Greater Philadelphia Regional Review*, Spring 2003, p. 10.

2. Robert Weissbourd and Christopher Berry, "The Changing Dynamics of Urban America," CEOs for Cities and RW Ventures, Chicago, March 30, 2004, p. 32.

CONCLUSION

1. Judith Rodin, "Aging and Health: Effects of the Sense of Control," *Science*, 233, no. 4770 (1986): 1271–1276. Judith Rodin, Christine Timko, and Susan Harris, "The Construct of Control: Biological and Psychosocial Correlates," in Carl Eisdorfer, M. Powell Lawton, and George L. Maddox (eds.), *Annual Review of Gerontology and Geriatrics* (New York: Springer, 1985), pp. 3–55.

2. Douglas C. Henton, John Melville, and Kimberly Walesh, *Civic Revolutionaries: Igniting the Passion for Change in America's Communities* (San Francisco: Jossey-Bass, 2004).

INDEX

ACKNOWLEDGMENTS

The work described in this book, the West Philadelphia Initiatives, could not have taken place without the extraordinary vision, commitment, and support of the University of Pennsylvania Board of Trustees. Board chairs Roy Vagelos and James Riepe, the Trustee Committees on Neighborhood Initiatives, led by Gilbert Casellas, and on Facilities, led by William Mack, were creative partners and extremely generous with their time and their expertise. Bill Mack's experience as a leading real-estate investor and developer helped us through many complex negotiations and projects, and we owe him an enormous debt.

The members of Penn's senior leadership team were heroic in the time, energy, and commitment they gave to this work. Early in the Initiatives John Fry, executive vice president, and Steve Schutt, vice president and chief of staff, truly had two full-time jobs, and none of the Initiatives could have happened without them. Both went on to become college presidents and both are continuing brilliant work in their communities. Omar Blaik, senior vice president for facilities and real-estate services, took over for John and led an explosion of activity. He is an urban visionary whose taste and imprint are on so much of what now looks best and works best in the neighborhood. The four of us did everything from picking fabrics and paint colors for new buildings, developing retail establishments, planning schools, and negotiating contracts. We also shared sleepless nights over safety. They were great partners.

I am also grateful to all the other University officers who made the Initiatives such a high priority, despite the other demands on their time: Carol Scheman, vice president for government, community, and public affairs, and Glenn Bryan, director of city and community relations, were deeply involved in every element but were on point tirelessly for all aspects of community and government consultation and collaboration. They attended to the countless approvals needed, the thorny neighborhood relations, the numerous block associations. Leroy Nunnery, vice president for business services, was key in the efforts concerning purchasing and economic development for neighborhood businesses and was a forceful advocate and generous mentor. Maureen Rush, vice president for public safety, was a driving force behind the plans for linking community- and campus-safety efforts. She was a tough cop and a warm community leader, filling a very difficult role with grace. Tom Lussenhop and Jack Shannon were John Fry's right and left hands in the early days of the work, and each has gone on to lead huge community-development efforts elsewhere in the country.

The dean of the Graduate School of Education, Susan Fuhrman, and the dean of Penn Design, Gary Hack, also played crucial roles in the West Philadelphia Initiatives. Susan led the efforts in the schools generally and planned the Penn Alexander School with Nancy Streim, her associate dean. When the three of us attended the first eighth-grade graduation together, there wasn't a dry eye among us. Gary was active in the overall master planning process and in architect selection for all of these projects. His expert judgment and firm hand guided us throughout the work. Ira Harkavy's brilliant work in the West Philadelphia schools was also key to the success of the Initiatives. Too many faculty were involved to thank everyone individually, but special recognition is due Eugenie Birch, David Brownlee, Dennis Culhane, and Laurie Olin for their extraordinary efforts. Lucy Kerman in the President's Office worried every detail and helped to pursue private-donor and foundation funding for some of the projects.

There were special partners in the community: first and foremost our councilwoman, Jannie Blackwell. We relied on her belief that everyone could come together and benefit together. She had the clout, the credibility, and the votes, and she always made things happen. Mayors Ed Rendell and John Street were fantastic supporters, and they tasked many departments in both their administrations to work with us, especially Planning, Licensing and Inspection, Economic Development, and the Philadelphia Industrial Development Corporation. Sheila Sydnor, principal of the Penn Alexander School, Barry Grossbach, long-time community resident and activist, the Reverend William Shaw, who chaired the Economic Inclusion Advisory Committee, and Paul Steinke, head of the University City District, were all crucial partners.

As the work developed it seemed important to document and evaluate it. I am grateful to John Kromer and Lucy Kerman for taking on this task. In this book I rely heavily on their report, *West Philadelphia Initiatives: A Case Study in Urban Revitalization.*

Jane Brooks worked on the early drafting of the book and interviewed all of the following individuals: Jannie Blackwell, Omar Blaik, Glenn Bryan, Gilbert Casellas, Pat Clancy, Dennis Culhane, John Fry, Kate Ward Gaus, Barry Grosbach, Ira Harkavy, Lindsay Johnson, Lucy Kerman, Mark Frazier Lloyd, Tom Lussenhop, Maureen Rush, Carol Scheman, Steve Schutt, Jack Shannon, Paul Steinke, Nancy Streim, Sheila Sydnor, Judy Wicks, and D-L Wormley. I am grateful to Jane for her probing interviews, analysis of written reports, and her creative writing. Karen Beck Pooley helped with reviews of the urban-planning material, and Eugenie Birch critically read early drafts and provided insight and encouragement. I am grateful to my assistants Michael Marco and Louise Lopez for helping their technology-challenged boss through her many pages of handwritten edits.

Finally, thanks to the Rockefeller Foundation for giving me the time, while in my new job as president of the foundation, to complete this book. Much of the final work was done at Rockefeller's Bellagio Study Center. The foundation's outstanding commitment to working communities has had tremendous impact on improving the lives of poor and vulnerable people in American cities.

And, as always, love to my husband, Paul, and son, Alex, with special thanks for their enthusiasm about the West Philadelphia Initiatives and my desire to write this book.